Advance Praise from Parents

66 I laughed throughout this book, because it's nice to know I'm not the only one who reacts instead of handling situations appropriately. I also cried, because I feel extremely inadequate when it comes to raising my kids. Your words perfectly fit my emotions.

Tammi R.

66 I read the first chapter and was immediately impressed. I have a one-year-old and don't want to fall into the trap of yelling and bribing as I see so many of our friends doing. Thank you.

Amy P.

66 I bought *ScreamFree Parenting* a couple of days ago and it's already paying huge dividends for me. Last week, my teenage daughter was coming home from California, and she had a choice about when she wanted to return. She opted to take the last flight of the day in order to stay a little longer with her friends. I explained this would mean she'd be very tired for school the next morning and she said she understood.

I'd been having trouble getting her up for school regularly, and the yelling had been getting old and going nowhere. Well, Monday morning I went to her room and said, "I'm leaving in 15 minutes - you're either in the car or I'm leaving you here and you can take an unexcused absence at school." 14 minutes later, she hopped in the car.

THANK YOU!!

This is a dream come true for my husband. We all need to calm down more in our lives and you've shown us the light. Thank you for already changing our lives in a matter of days.

Sincerely,
Lisa O.

66 I just wanted you to know, we have already started to apply what we are learning. We have two teenage children, and IT IS WORKING. I can't believe it. I am going to read the book again to make sure I haven't missed anything. You have made us feel very good about getting these teenagers through driving, dating and all of their trials, in a completely different way than we started out. We are much calmer as a husband and a wife and as a father and a mother. Thanks again.

Agnes G.

---

66 I just read the first chapter and was blown away. I am really hooked and can't wait to read more. When I can I get my hands on this. I have a tweny-one-month-old and I'm definitely familiar with the Waffle House scene. Please let me know when it will be on the shelves.

You're amazing,
Sally I.

---

66 I would describe myself briefly as a calm, cool, easy-going, humor-loving person but with three exceptions: an eleven-year-old, eight-year-old, and five-year-old. I would love to show my kids more of that side of me, but frustration arises inside and I have these knee-jerk reactions.

I have good kids, I really do, and I am trying with great zeal to raise them with good character quality; I cringe at the side of me that is squelching their memories of seeing a godly and "fun" mom. There is nobody else on God's earth that I would treat that disrespectfully, but my own kids . . . WHY?

I was brought up the same way that I find myself speaking and I hate it. I know it and I'm wanting that to change. I look forward to ordering your book because along with prayer and God's guidance I am hoping for a breakthrough into dealing with my own child issues in a more calming manner. Thank you.

May God Bless your mission!

Sincerely,
Karrin S.

PS. My sister and I share this battle together. It's not that we had awful parents, but there was no blessing associated to their parenting. it's interesting how the circle keeps going and you have to work so hard to break it!

" Thanks to this book, I am now asking myself whether I am being reactive or calm. It is a good question to ask yourself frequently to get you to a good starting point. I appreciate what you are doing.

And after reading of the four levels of love in Chapter Eleven, I have found a common thread of why I have gotten involved with the people that I have. I have been able to examine myself and my reasons and have come out of the microscope with a renewed sense of courage that I can do this by myself (I am a single parent) and I can do just fine. Sometimes, especially when I'm tired, I want someone else to "do it for me." But that one little phrase, "I love me for your benefit," makes me feel empowered and that I can do this. I don't NEED help from someone else regarding being a parent myself. I appreciate it if it's there, but I can get by without it. Anyway, thanks for your inspiration and caring for people you don't even know. I appreciate it.

Robyn S.

" I am the single parent of three children, ages fifteen, thirteen, and five. And ScreamFree Parenting was an absolute treat to read. I have so many friends that I would like to give this to! The flow of the book was great. I was gently guided from one precept or principle to the next. I was certainly challenged to look at myself throughout the book, but in a compassionate and humorous way--no judgment. There was no sense that the author was looking down at me, the struggling idiot. There was a genuine sense that he was connected to me, the reader . . . he was just a fellow traveler that happened to be further down the road. Hal's experience as a coach was delightfully evident. He validated, acknowledged, reframed, probed, educated, and championed the reader.

Learning that shifting the focus onto me (because it is always about me!) will eliminate the personalization of my children's behavior. When I personalize something, it becomes all about my ego, and my self-centered fears run wild! But by shining the light on this behavioral pattern while making me feel normal (thanks, Coach Hal!) I had a huge "Aha!" moment. I was inspired to practice these new principles with some wonderful results.

I have always wanted to be less of a dictator and more of a loving guide; this book has given me some fantastic tools to pursue that goal.

Thank you so much for the privilege of reading this book. I will continue to spread the Gospel according to ScreamFree, and wish you all the greatest success.

Sincerely (and much more calmly),
Lisa U.

66 I really, REALLY liked what I read about the ScreamFree approach. It's easy to see why you are so gung-ho about this movement. I found myself thinking, "I sure wish my parents had read this book when they were raising me! I'd be saving a TON of money in therapy right now! . . . " :)

It's just such a thoughtful, holistic approach. I'm not a parent, but I could see right away how helpful the principles could be in my marriage and other significant relationships. It occurs to me how many people never learn the principles in the book—and so their relationships stay at really reduced levels of emotional maturity. It's exciting to see the receipt this teaching is getting, and to think about the relationships that will be immensely helped by it.

Thanks for letting me be part of this.
Cindy M.

---

66 *ScreamFree Parenting* is a good reminder that yelling really accomplishes nothing. I come from a family of yellers, so we are now aware of yelling at the kids. The worst part is that the kids pick it up real fast. Liked the story about the Waffle House.

Tim D.

---

66 I loved this book and have already applied some of the principles. They really work! I still scream occasionally, but not nearly as much (or as loud). We all seem to be a little calmer and quieter now. I deal with my kids as kids, not as adults or babies. By behaving the way I want my kids to behave: quietly, calmly and confidently, we do a lot less struggling and a lot more cuddling.

Johna P.

scream \\'skrēm\ :
to get emotionally reactive with your kids; can take a number
of forms, including raising your voice, orbiting your life around
theirs, cutting yourself off to avoid watching their mistakes (and
then telling them "I told you so"), trying to control their behavior
and feelings, or sacrificing yourself for your family and then
resenting them when they don't appreciate all your efforts.

ScreamFree™ \\'skrēm'frē\ :
learning to relate with your kids in a calm, cool, and
*conn*ected way, taking hold of your own emotional responses no
matter how your children choose to behave; learning to focus on
yourself and take care of yourself for your family's benefit, giving
your children the best chance to grow into self-directed adults.

SCREAMFREE™
PARENTING

Raising Your Kids by Keeping Your Cool

Hal Edward Runkel, LMFT

ScreamFree Parenting:

Raising Your Kids by Keeping Your Cool

OAKMONT
PUBLISHING

Published by Oakmont Publishing, LLC

2180 Satellite Blvd., Suite 400

Duluth, GA 30097

www.screamfree.com

©2005 ScreamFree Parenting, LLC

All rights reserved.

Typesetting by Fritz Miller Studios, Inc., www.fritzmiller.com

Printed in the United States of America

ISBN 09759981-1-0

To Jenny,
of course.

And for Hannah and Brandon,
I'm thinking two things about you . . .

Table of Contents

How to Read This Book   i

Section One

Becoming the "Cool" Parent Your Kids Really Need   1

1   Parenting Is Not About Kids, It's About Parents   7

2   Growing Up Is Hard to Do, Especially for Grown-Ups   23

3   If You're Not under Control,

       Then You Cannot Be in Charge   37

       Storytime   51

Section Two

Keeping Your Cool Means Creating *Space*   57

4   Begin with the End in Mind,

       but Let Go of the Final Results   61

5   Kids Need Their Room   77

6   Resistance Is Futile; Practice Judo Parenting   95

7   You Are Not a Prophet (and Neither Is Grandma)   113

       Storytime   129

Section Three

Keeping Your Cool Means Creating a *Place*   133

8 Parents Set the Table by Setting the Tone

    (and Vice Versa)   137

9 Let the Consequences Do the Screaming   153

10 Empty Threats Are Really Broken Promises   169

Storytime   183

Section Four

Putting Yourself into Practice   187

11 Put on Your Own Oxygen Mask First   191

12 Revolutionary Relationships   209

Acknowledgments   223

How to Read This Book

My goal for this book is the same for my company: **to calm the world, one relationship at a time, beginning with yours.** In particular, I hope to inspire you toward revolutionizing your relationships with each of your children. I firmly believe that by incorporating these principles into your way of life, you will begin to enjoy the types of parent-child relationships you have always craved. These are relationships full of joy, cooperation, harmony, and most of all, mutual respect. Peace in your family is not as far off as you might think.

In order for this book to help you pursue those relationships, I have sought to provide a structure that logically introduces you to the ScreamFree way, one step at a time. At first, some of these principles may seem different, for they run counter to a lot of popular teaching. So while you may feel tempted to skim the table of contents and skip forward to a section or chapter that catches your eye, you will get the most out of the book by reading each section consecutively.

The book is divided into four sections, with multiple chapters in each section. At the conclusion of each section, I will tell a true story from the real life experiences of my coaching and/or therapy clients. I am honored and privileged to work with some of the most courageous people in the world, folks who choose to invest their time, money, and significant emotional energy toward learning to focus on themselves. Walking alongside them in this journey and watching them revolutionize their relationships in the process is my undeserved blessing. It is why I do what I do.

Each of these stories is a remarkable testimony to the power of ScreamFree Parenting. Of course, the names and details have been altered to protect client confidentiality, but the events are all true—and powerful. I have selected each of these particular stories because they wonderfully illustrate the principles of the preceding section. As you will see, these stories represent parent-child relationships in various stages of life. While everyone's story is different, I know you can find yourself in here somewhere.

Above all, take whatever from this book that inspires you to revolutionize your relationships and discard the rest. You do not have to accept all that I say in order to enjoy the types of relationships you crave or become the type of parent you desire to be. Please email me at feedback@screamfree.com, and let me know how this book intersects with your life. I look forward to hearing from you about your journey with ScreamFree Parenting. Your feedback helps provide the inspiration I use to continue on this journey to calm the world.

Finally, let me offer a brief word about my spiritual background, and thus, the spiritual background of this material. I consider myself firmly entrenched in the Judeo-Christian tradition, and I believe that the ScreamFree message is ultimately God's message. I believe God is the original ScreamFree Parent to us all, and his way of relating with himself and with others is the model I teach and try to live. These ScreamFree principles are biblical principles, both from the Hebrew Bible and the Christian New Testament. With all that stated, this is not meant to be an explicitly Judeo-Christian book. You do not have to convert to any reli-gious tradition in order to live as a ScreamFree Parent. You will see in Chapter Eleven, however, that I do believe developing your spir-itual relationship with God is the best way to love yourself and your family. But again, I want you to take whatever from this book that inspires you to revolutionize your relationships, and discard the rest. You do not need to believe all that I believe, spiritual or otherwise, in order to have great relationships with your kids.

All you have to do, you will see, is learn to keep your cool.

Section One

Becoming the "Cool" Parent
Your Kids Really Need

Parents can tell but never teach,
unless they practice what they preach.
—Arnold H. Glasgow

In raising my children, I have lost my mind
but found my soul.
—Lisa T. Shepherd

Every kid wants to have "cool" parents. No, this does not
mean they want parents who try to be hip to the latest styles
(this makes you decidedly *un*cool). And contrary to some popular teaching, being a cool parent does not mean being so
permissive that you let your kids do whatever they want. What
every kid wants are parents who can keep their cool, even when
things get hot. Especially when things get hot. Kids want par-

1

ents who are far less anxious and far more levelheaded than they are. Your kids want you to remain unflappable, even when they flip out.

As it turns out, that's exactly what they need.

Parents everywhere are facing the toughest challenge of their lives: trying to create a loving family environment filled with mutual respect and cooperation. And they're trying to do this in a culture that celebrates irresponsibility and self-indulgence. It's no wonder parents feel more anxious than ever before. They feel overwhelmed and underappreciated. And I believe they all want help.

I believe parents are searching for someone to present an inspiring vision of how it all could be different. We have heard all sorts of packaged programs delivering fail-proof techniques to raise perfect children. We've heard about the countless failures of the past two generations while at the same time hearing of the urgent need to return to the good ol' days. And most of all, we have been bombarded with the call to sacrifice ourselves for the sake of our kids, focus all of our attention on what our kids need, and learn to always be there for them.

We've heard all of this and more, and it's not helping. This call is actually hurting, leaving parents feeling more overwhelmed, more frustrated, and less capable.

So, what's wrong? Or better yet, what's the right direction out of this mess? A few years ago, a brilliant family therapist and rabbi named Edwin Friedman asked a critical question: When's the last time you saw a parenting book telling parents to focus less on their children?

Well, this may be the first you've ever seen. *ScreamFree Parenting* may be the first book you've read that tells all parents to stop orbiting their lives around their children and return the focus to themselves.

So is that the problem, that we're too focused on our kids? Absolutely. In a rash reaction to the "children should be seen and not heard" formula, we have gone to another extreme, the "our lives revolve around our children" formula. Just look at us chauffeuring our kids from school to practice to yet another practice in a minivan with stickers plastered all over it. And whose name is on these stickers? Whose name is on this minivan we paid for? Whether it be an honor student badge or a soccer ball, our kids' names tell the world who really owns the vehicle. And our lives. And it's not good for them or us.

> I believe parents are searching for someone to present an inspiring vision of how it all could be different.

ScreamFree Parenting provides a way out of this mess, a way to restore both parent and child to their rightful places in the home.

So Why ScreamFree?

Not all of us scream at our kids. Not all of us struggle with keeping our cool. But all parents do experience, to various levels or degrees, a universal struggle. We all feel incredibly anxious and we don't know what to do about it. We feel anxious about our kids and their choices. We fret and worry about how our kids will turn out. Inevitably, we're so focused on our kids that we don't realize when this anxiety takes over—and we get reactive.

ScreamFree Parenting is about calming all of our reactive responses to this anxiety. It's called ScreamFree because screaming is the most popular reaction. But there are other reactions, like disconnecting ourselves from the situation. Or beginning to overcompensate (ever pick up after your kids because you're so tired of battling them about it?). Some of us just give up and keep giving in.

> **Your number one leadership role in your family is that of a *calming authority*.**

All of these reactions are just different ways of screaming. And they are all just as ineffective in creating the type of relationships we crave with our children. But there is hope. There is a better way.

What I offer in this book is a way for you to envision yourself in a non-reactive, yet fully-connected relationship with each of your children. And that's the catch—remaining both calm and connected. Many parents can remain calm by simply disengaging from the relationship. Other parents stay fully engaged, only to let their anxiety drive the relationship. ScreamFree Parenting teaches you to calm your own anxiety first, enabling you to remain fully connected and involved. And this creates a revolutionary relationship with each of your kids and the rest of your family—a relationship where your position is that of an inspiring influence; a relationship where your number one leadership role in the family is that of a calming authority. Regardless of the ages of your children and regardless of the mistakes you've made up to this point, you can restore yourself to this position in the family.

You can, by learning to focus on yourself, begin to make changes in the way you parent, changes that dramatically change the entire makeup of your family. You can, beginning today, start practicing the principles that will bring about new patterns of connection and cooperation. Such changes won't be easy and they won't come automatically. Becoming a ScreamFree Parent involves a difficult journey, facing difficult truths about yourself and your relationships. Difficult, but not impossible. And it's not all tough stuff, either—becoming a ScreamFree Parent also invites you to treat yourself better than you've ever thought you could or should.

It all begins with one fundamental shift. As you will see, parenting is not about children, it's about parents.

Chapter One

Parenting Is Not About Kids,
It's About Parents

It's not you, it's me.
—George Costanza, *Seinfeld*

The greatest thing you can do for your kids is learn to focus on
yourself.

This statement might not make complete sense right away. It
might, in fact, be downright offensive. What? Turn the focus away
from my children and onto myself? Isn't that against all the rules?

No, it isn't. I'm not proposing that you put your children last
on the list. Far from it. What I'm saying is that by focusing on
yourself, you will have a healthier, happier relationship with your
whole family.

7

You see, most of us have been operating with a faulty model of how to live in our relationships. That's not to say our relationships are all faulty, but the model sure is. We've been operating with a model that says in order to have healthy relationships, we need to focus on meeting other people's needs, trying to serve them and make them happy. To even question such a model draws controversy, I know, but stay with me.

This book is going to talk about why this model is so faulty, particularly in our parent-child relationships. For now, there are a few simple things we should consider. First, it's a given that there are things in this world we can control and things we cannot control. Now ask yourself this question: how smart is it to focus your energy on something you can't do anything about, something you cannot control? Answer: Not very. Follow-up question: Which category do your kids fall into? In other words, are your children something you can control or something you cannot control? Here's an even tougher question: Even if you could control your kids, should you? Is that what parenting is all about? And what if it's not the kids who are out of control?

> By focusing on yourself, you will have a healthier, happier relationship with your whole family.

Who's Really Out of Control Here?

Waffle House seemed like a good idea that Saturday morning. My kids, Hannah and Brandon, were four and two at the time. My lovely wife Jenny and I had a busy day ahead of us and breakfast is the most important meal of the day. Why not have a nice family breakfast together?

The first Waffle House we walked into was just too full, but, thankfully, there is no shortage of Waffle Houses in suburban Atlanta. So, we piled back into the car, strapped our children into their car seats, quieted disappointed whines with promises of lots of maple syrup, and drove the hundred yards or so to the second Waffle House. And the line there was just as long as the first one.

There was no way we were getting the kids back into the car for another trip, so we decided to just wait it out. They had crayons and paper for the kids. My wife and I could even get in a little adult conversation. A win-win situation.

As if that weren't enough, a sign caught my eye. If my children drew a picture, they were entitled to a paper Waffle House hat—just like the grill man wears—and a free waffle. Sometimes life is good. The kids colored. My wife and I talked. The time flew and before we knew it, we were seated—my wife and daughter on one side of the booth, my son and I on the other. They brought the kids their paper hats and I even tried one on.

If you've never been to a Waffle House, you would be amazed at the consistency of their architecture. All the tables surround the kitchen and wall-length windows surround the tables. It's very open, and it's easy to notice the goings on of others.

Now, while I was feeling pretty good by this time, my kids hadn't eaten anything all morning. Hungry kids who've done nothing but wait around can be . . . restless. My four-year-old handled it all right, just the garden-variety complaints. But my two-year-old son sure was feeling two years old, if you know what I mean. Two-year-olds generally have no regard for things like "practicing an inside voice" or "using words like a big boy" when they've been forced in and out of a car with nothing but promises to eat. Cooperating with me was not high on his list of priorities at the time. Enjoying a nice family breakfast didn't seem like such a good idea now.

But I'm a licensed marriage and family therapist. I'm a relationship coach. I know how to control myself and keep from losing my temper. I know better than to react and resort to yelling and violent acts of coercion. I can stay calm in the face of increasing levels of anxiety. But then my son threw his fork on the floor. My resolve began to fade.

The fork made a loud noise, causing all the people around us to look at me. Some of them even pointed and whispered (at least that's what it felt like they were doing). I looked over at my perfect wife sitting there with my perfect daughter. There is an unwritten rule among parents with multiple kids: Whoever is sitting on your side is on your watch. So while the women in my life are enjoying this angelic scene of cooperation and intimacy, my son and I are on the verge of World War III.

Still, I am the expert on human relationships. I'm the one planning to write a book someday called *ScreamFree Parenting*. Was I going to allow a two-year-old to push my buttons? You bet I was. See, the fork got such a great response, my son began to wonder what might happen if he threw his waffle—plate and all—on the floor.

Here's what might happen: Daddy might lose his cool! And that's precisely what did happen.

I snatched him up and stormed out of the restaurant. All eyes were fixed on us as my son started to scream. And kick. And hit. I was seething as I pushed the door open with such force it rattled the glass walls. The reverberating structure got everyone's attention. The entire restaurant saw me yelling at my son, using big words, asking rhetorical questions, puffing out my chest, pointing my finger and intimidating a boy who couldn't have stood more than thirty-six inches tall. What a big man I was!

After the ugly scene was over, Brandon and I returned to our seats to complete our nice family breakfast. And there sat Jenny, my loving and faithful wife. I think she wanted to say something supportive and reassuring, but she just couldn't contain the smirk. I was a volcano looking for an excuse to erupt.

"What?" I barked.

"Nice hat."

It was then I realized the paper Waffle House hat still sat squarely on top of my head. The entire scene had taken place with a silly hat on top of a silly explosion from a silly man who wanted more than anything to be taken seriously.

Our Biggest Enemy as Parents

Truth be told, I didn't need the hat to make me look foolish. I had done that myself with my knee-jerk reactivity. In fact, that kind of emotional reaction is our worst enemy when it comes to having great relationships.

Let me say that again: *emotional reactivity is our worst enemy when it comes to having great relationships.*

If you don't get anything else from this book, get this: our biggest struggle as parents is not with the television; it's not with bad influences; it's not even with drugs or alcohol. Our biggest struggle as parents is with our own emotional reactivity. That's why the greatest thing we can do for our kids is learn to focus on us, not them. Let's concentrate on what we can control—calming our own emotional, knee-jerk reactions.

What's so damaging about being too reactive? Keep reading. The next couple of chapters will make it clear. For now, consider this: how can we have any influence on our children's decision-making if we don't have an influence on our own? When we get reactive, we get regressive. That is, we shrink back to an immature level of functioning. Think of me at Waffle House. I became just as immature as my two-year-old in an effort to get him to act more mature than I.

How effective can that be? I've come to realize that I may get compliance eventually, but at what price? I may have screamed my son into submission at Waffle House, but what type of relationship will I have with him if I continue to parent by reactive intimidation?

If we want to be influential, then we have to first bring ourselves under control. Only then can we choose our response. Only then can we choose how we want to behave, regardless of how our children choose to behave.

So if emotional reactivity is our biggest enemy, where does it come from? More importantly, what can we do about it? Most of us cannot think of a more terrifying emotion than feeling overwhelmed. We can feel scared, exhausted, worried or angry, but nothing shuts us down, stops us in our tracks and causes us to throw up our hands in futility like feeling overwhelmed. When we feel incapable of coping with, handling or accomplishing all we have to do, we are overwhelmed. When it seems like even if we weren't so tired and so frustrated we still couldn't keep all the plates spinning, that's about as scary as it gets. When we feel stretched beyond our limits, that's when we just want to quit.

And I can think of no more accurate description of how most of us parents feel. Far too often, we feel overwhelmed. We feel over-stretched, over-committed, under-prepared and under-appreciated. That's a recipe for feeling overwhelmed. As a result, most of us feel a gnawing sense of inadequacy. We don't just feel like bad parents, we feel like failures.

Unfortunately, this is the one area of life where we cannot afford to fail. If there is one area where we feel the pressure of absolute success, it is with our parenting. After all, we are bombarded with messages about the importance of time with our kids, involvement in our kids' lives, and putting our family first

> Parents feel over-stretched, over-committed, under-prepared, and under-appreciated.

among our priorities. Magazine racks are crammed with new parenting techniques and advice. Studies consistently show the ill effects of bad parenting. Our churches preach the need to put families first. With all of this pressure comes just more fear and feelings of inadequacy.

And then there's the most intense pressure of all. We know that how we do as parents will reverberate throughout history. We are raising the next generation, and they will either continue the success and progress of past generations or they will erase it all.

Anyone feeling overwhelmed?

Parenting is serious business. The stakes are unbelievably high. The cost of failure is unimaginable. I know you feel the intense weight of performing as a parent. You may wonder if you're the only one who sometimes feels inadequate, even inept. You may wonder, Is it supposed to be this hard? The answer is Yes. And No. Yes, parenting is hard and it's supposed to be. We'll get to that in the next chapter. But no, we don't have to feel this much pressure. We don't have to feel overwhelmed.

The Most Damaging Lie About Parenting

The reason we feel so overwhelmed is because most of us are attempting to follow an impossible model. Here is the most damaging lie about parenting: We are responsible *for* our children.

Most people would define parenting like this: "It is our job as parents to get our children to think, feel, and especially, behave like a good person. It is our job to get our children to be good." Right?

Wrong.

Now, let me be clear. In my experience working with families, I've seen the devastating effects of terrible parenting on now-grown adults. Certainly we have a profound amount of influence on how our kids turn out. This book will illustrate the power we have to shape our children. In fact, I don't think we can overestimate this influence we have on future generations.

But what that really means is that we have a far greater responsibility TO our children than we have FOR our children. Let me say that again, so it will sink in. We are much less responsible *for* our children than we've ever been told. However, we have a far greater responsibility *to* our children than we've ever realized.

Most of us feel like we're responsible *for* our children. Sure, they're totally dependent on us right from the beginning. But let's think about that for a moment. If we are responsible *for* our children, then we have a really big problem. How long did it take you to realize that your child had a mind of her own? Early on they start to make their own choices. This is part of growing up. In truth, this *is* growing up. Even in their infancy our kids start to embrace their God-given ability to make decisions about what they will and will not do. They begin to choose how they feel, how they think, and how they behave.

I know this is simplistic, but this concept carries all the seeds of our frustration in raising kids. They simply make different choices than we want them to make! They choose to yell and scream at the grocery store. They choose not to do their homework. They choose to break curfew and disrespect our rules. They choose to throw their waffles on the floor in front of a restaurant full of people!

If you are responsible *for* your children, then you have to figure out how to program them to make the "right" choices. And you need to do it quickly. You have to learn the right techniques to get them to think, feel, and behave according to your definition of "good."

All of this sounds alarmingly like obedience training. It comes as no surprise, then, to find parenting books at your local bookseller written by animal trainers! "What works for Fido can work for your child!"

If you're totally responsible *for* coercing your children into being good, then it makes perfect sense to enlist some program or system like that. I, for one, cannot imagine our Creator wants us to treat children like animals. Such an approach may make parents feel big and in charge, but it leaves children feeling small and incompetent.

The fact that our children have been given the power of choice, as self-directed human beings, can thwart even the best obedience-training program. Children will soon realize they are in a no-win situation. Either they kill their own decision-making spirit in an attempt to reduce their parents' anxiety, or they rebel against their parents' authority. That's the catch-22 of the "responsibility *for*" model of parenting. Parents either program their children correctly or they have failed. Children either conform to the system and surrender their individuality or they rebel against it.

Do you see the two categories we have neatly set up? On one hand, we have "What Will Make Mom and Dad Less Anxious" and on the other hand we have "Wrong Choices That Will Make Mom and Dad More Anxious." For most families, there simply is no third option. In this system, there isn't the possibility of children learning to act for themselves and think critically about their choices. Doing so would equal rebellion. If your child ends up "doing the right thing," then you've raised a robot. But if your child ends up thinking and acting for himself, then you've raised a rebel.

There Is a Better Way

But there has to be another way—a way to say yes to our profound influence on our children's lives without taking total responsibility for those lives. There must be a way to dramatically influence the life of a child without resorting to programming and coercion. I call this third option ScreamFree Parenting, because it emphasizes a radical focus on calming our own anxiety.

Not all of us scream at our children, but all of us struggle with reactive behaviors. We may scream, we may manipulate, we may even use violence. On the other hand, we may neglect, we may avoid, we may even withhold love. All of these are different examples of emotional reactivity. And as I said before, they are all just different ways of screaming. ScreamFree Parenting takes all of this incredibly seriously and says the only way to retain a position of influence with our children is to regain a position of control over ourselves.

Initially, this might feel or sound self-centered. It may even sound like self-indulgent navel-gazing. I promise you, it is not. If you stick with me through the first part of this book, you'll see that this is all designed to make you far less selfish and far more mature in your parenting. The bottom line is this: You need to be in control of the things you *can* control, and that starts (and may end) with you.

You're responsible *to* your children, your spouse, your friends and family members. You're accountable *to* them for how you think, feel, and behave towards them.

I want you to actually say this out loud: "I am responsible *to* my child for how I relate with my child."

Again, the focus is on you because you are the only one you can ultimately control. If you make sure you behave—even when your kids misbehave—then you have a greater chance of positively influencing the situation, any situation. This is ScreamFree Parenting.

In this book you'll read several stories of parents facing the very situations you face. They range from the ordinary, like the struggles of getting a baby to sleep through the night, to the dramatic, like the "we have your teenage son in custody" scenario we all dread. All these situations create anxiety, sometimes the intense, "I don't know if I can handle this" type of anxiety. And that's okay.

This book will help you face similar situations, whether your kids are tots or teenagers, with a renewed confidence in your own integrity. Becoming a ScreamFree Parent involves a growing self-awareness, a greater sense of self-direction, and an increased willingness to take personal responsibility for your actions, regardless of the actions of those around you.

> The only way to retain a position of influence with our children is to regain a position of control over ourselves.

Come to think of it, isn't that what we want for our kids? We want them to be self-aware, self-directed and able to take personal responsibility for their actions. But they will never get there if we don't model it all for them. You see, this parenting stuff is more about us than it is about them.

The first idea in this book is: "The greatest thing you can do for your kids is learn to focus on yourself." Getting rid of the weight of the "responsibility *for*" model is the first step. For the rest of the book, we will turn our focus toward all that's involved in your responsibility *to* your children.

This will not be an easy journey. Once you turn the focus inward, you always learn more about yourself than you want to know. Like how easily you allow access to your emotional buttons, hoping others just "don't go there." Or how much you've been trying to teach your children lessons you have yet to learn. Turning your attention to yourself is not a self-indulgent journey once you open your eyes to see where you still need to grow. And that's what becoming ScreamFree is all about.

I would tell you to hold on to your hat, because it's going to be a bumpy ride. But then again, the last thing we need to do is keep wearing our silly hats.

Reflection Questions

1. The opening line of this chapter is "The greatest thing you can do for your kids is learn to focus on yourself." When you read that line for the first time, what was your initial reaction?

   that makes sense

2. How is that reaction any different now that you have read the chapter?

   It makes more sense

3. Recall one of the times you have felt your children were "out of control." If you had had greater control over your own emotions, how could the situation have had a different outcome?

   It wouldn't have lasted as long

4. In the past, what has prevented you from focusing on yourself? Fear of being self-centered? Fear of finding yourself in worse shape than you previously thought?

   Pride &

5. What do you think are your responsibilities *to* each of your children?

   - to be able to listen to them
   - follow through
   - more positive
   - to be consistent
   - more quality time

Chapter Two

Growing Up Is Hard to Do, Especially for Grown-Ups

Nobody said it was easy;
no one ever said it would be this hard.
—Coldplay, "The Scientist"

Child rearing myth: Labor ends
when the baby is born.
—Unknown

I have always hated the phrase "No pain, no gain."

Actually, I only hate it when someone else says it to me. It's rarely said in a nurturing and hopeful sort of way. It usually means, "Stop your whining!" I usually hear it when I'm under a barbell at the gym wondering if my insurance covers exercise accidents.

I actually like "No pain, no gain" when I get to say it to someone else, like my wife or my buddies or my kids. That way I get to be the one standing above them, dispensing from on high the wisdom I've accumulated through my years of personal struggle. I get to relish watching all the "productive" pain they now have to endure.

The truth is, "No pain, no gain" has a lot of truth to it. Pain is often the greatest catalyst to powerful change. Think of the way we build muscle. By intentionally inducing pain and tension in a controlled environment, we add size, strength, and endurance. But there is a catch. The proverb is only true—it only has actual power to change our lives—when we can say it to ourselves. A coach, a teacher, a personal trainer, or even an author like me can say it and believe it, but until you incorporate it into your core beliefs, into your very bones, it will do nothing but frustrate you. It's only when you say it, repeat it, and believe it yourself that it becomes a true catalyst for change.

> Pain is often the greatest catalyst to powerful change.

That's what makes this chapter so challenging for me to write and, very possibly, for you to read. If I wrote this as if I were your personal family guru doling out wisdom from some mountaintop, then you would have nothing but a handful of pithy sayings. I would have failed to teach you anything about your life and your parenting. The only way for this to work is for our conversation to inspire you to inspire yourself. And that can only happen if we tell the truth.

First, let us reaffirm what you already know about being a parent: it's probably the most challenging thing you've ever done. Let us also reaffirm, however, what you hope about being a parent: that it can be the most rewarding experience you've ever imagined.

So, we have a good news-bad news scenario. The bad news is parenting is hard. Nothing you learn in this book will make that go away. The good news is parenting is rewarding. No pain, no gain. But reading it here won't make it become a reality until you're ready to believe it and act on it.

Growing Pains

Parenting is painful at times, and you already know it's really difficult. But what you might not know is that parenting is supposed to be that way. Why? Parenting is a growth process, that's why. And nothing has ever grown without feeling some sort of growing pains. A saying attributed to Jesus takes it even further, stating no seed can bear fruit unless it first dies in the ground. No wonder it feels like this parenting thing is gonna kill me!

In many ways, you have already experienced a sort of death. When you became a parent, so much of the life you knew disappeared. Think about it. It has to be a verifiable fact that every parent has uttered this exact question: What did I do with all my free time before I had this child!?! Your free time, your sleep patterns, your spending habits, your travel plans, your friendships, your marriage—everything changed forevermore. No matter what happens from now on, you will never *not* be a parent. You will never be the same as you were before kids. And that can sometimes feel like a death.

And it can also feel like a rebirth. Just as this new baby is born and delivered into our care, so we begin a new, radical growth process of our own. Both child and parent are in this growth process together; both are facing new challenges as they relate to one another.

For parents, the difference is that we are responsible for setting the parameters of the relationship. In other words, it's up to us to shape the rules of how to handle the inherent anxiety involved in such a close relationship. How we handle our growing pains will directly influence how the rest of the family handles their growing pains.

In his remarkable books, Dr. David Schnarch urges us to think of all relationships as people-growing machines. I believe this is especially true when it comes to parenting. Nothing else demands that we grow in patience and support skills as much as being a parent. No other situation requires as much consistency. Nowhere else do we feel quite as vulnerable and unqualified as when we are faced with the task of helping a needy and dependent child become a self-directed adult.

Part of being a grown-up, though, is the willingness to endure discomfort now for the sake of a payoff later. So, what's the payoff? Maturity, both for our children and for ourselves. And, as you'll see throughout this book, seeking our own maturity makes for a vibrant, stimulating, and mutually loving relationship with each of our children.

But that all depends on whether we choose to accept the difficulty of parenting as a challenge, an opportunity for our own growth. When we choose to grow, we can actually appreciate the fact that pain and anxiety can assist us to grow further. This increases the chances that we will approach parenting with a renewed focus on ourselves, not our children, as the number one agents for our own peace and contentment. The difficult times with our kids become *necessary* for our continued development; they now have meaning. Viewed in this light, our struggles are infused with purpose. As our perspective changes, we won't be nearly as tempted to resent these children our Creator has placed under our watch.

The Challenge of Reactivity

A coaching client of mine once witnessed a woman and her daughter at a local coffee shop. While waiting in line, the little girl kept hanging on a swinging employee's gate.

After repeated pleading (and numerous threats), the mother finally blurted out, "IF YOU DON'T LET GO OF THAT DOOR, I'M GOING TO EMBARRASS YOU IN FRONT OF ALL THESE PEOPLE!"

Ah, the irony. Like the "nice hat" episode I painfully recounted earlier, this story illustrates who really has something to be embarrassed about. That's the price of this kind of reactivity. And it's an epidemic. Just look around. How often do you see people get irrationally defensive? How often do you see parents give up, cave in, and check out?

> Part of being a grown-up is enduring discomfort now for the sake of a payoff later.

See if this sounds familiar. You've had one of those days at work, you somehow managed to get toner dust all over your new pants, and then you get a call from your daughter on her cell phone.

"Hey, Mom, where are you? You were supposed to be here half an hour ago."

Oops—today is your day to pick up the kids at school. You just want to get home and change clothes, but now you've got to rush over to the school. And you've got to get to the grocery store or it's pizza for the third night this week. You crank up the van and it's sitting on empty. Feeling the anxiety yet? You get to the store (without the shopping list because you forgot it back at the office) and the kids start the dreaded "Ws"—the Whining Wants. Once that starts, you start the "STOP ITs" and the "I SAID NOs".

Their Ws might subside for a bit as you bark at these darling angels, but the kids are every bit as stressed as you are—and they didn't choose to come to the store. When you finally get to the checkout line, your youngest can only see the shiny, sweet things placed exactly at her eye-level (brilliant marketing move or diabolical plot?) and the Whining Wants return. And, of course, the lady in front of you is paying with an out-of-state, two-party check and has a stack of coupons.

It seems your only choice is to either give in or flip out. Of course, if you give in to one kid, then the others go for the kill, even the older ones. And if you even think about saying "no" to one after you've said "yes" to another, be prepared for the fairness fight. Children discover the concept of equity early in life. More often than not, for most of us, the flip-out is inevitable, even after the give-in.

"STOP IT RIGHT NOW!"

"WHY CAN'T YOU TWO JUST BE QUIET? WE'LL BE HOME IN A MINUTE!"

"IF YOU DON'T LET GO OF THAT RIGHT NOW, I'M GOING TO EMBARRASS YOU IN FRONT OF ALL THESE PEOPLE!"

Sometimes these lovely terms of endearment are accompanied by the arm-yank, the ear-tug or the dreaded finger-wag. If it gets really heated, a head-slap or a neck-grab may even make an appearance.

Before Paul Reiser starred in the show Mad About You, he had one of the leading roles in a less popular show called My Two Dads, where he played the father of a teenage girl. Whenever I see a parent resorting to the finger-wagging technique of screaming, I remember the time Reiser's character was doing the same: lecturing his daughter whilst delivering a serious finger wagging.

But in the middle of the lecture he stopped himself, looked at his hand, and posed the question, "When did I grow my father's finger?"

All he needed was a silly paper hat.

We all know the definition of insanity, right? Doing the same thing over and over again, expecting a different result. Can you recall a time when you panicked and flipped out and it actually helped?

Usually, our reactivity causes the very outcome we most fear. And that's the price of reactivity. Count it as a rule of the universe—whenever we give in to our anxious reactivity, we help create the very outcome we're hoping to avoid.

Something that happened to me a few years ago provides a remarkable illustration of this rule. Thankfully, it also provides a remarkable illustration of the power of a nonreactive presence, which is what ScreamFree Parenting is all about.

An Opportunity for Growth

We bought our first house when our daughter, Hannah, was four years old. Our son, Brandon, had just turned two. The kids were fascinated with all of the newness—their rooms, the new playground in the backyard, and most of all, the steep staircase in the two-story foyer. The staircase was attached to one wall, leaving a long banister on the unattached side and nothing but hardwood floors below.

It took all of one day for Hannah to discover the thrill of climbing up the stairs on the *out*side of the banister. With just enough overhang to stand on and plenty of support pickets to hang on to, this banister provided an indoor climbing adventure. Thankfully, I noticed the expedition before she got in over my head. I told her to come down and instructed her that climbing the outside of the stairs was off-limits.

What I didn't notice, however, was Brandon watching his big sister's every move.

Two weeks later, I walked out of my bedroom at the top of the stairs to find my smiling, adorable son three-quarters of the way up the stairs, balancing on the few inches of overhang on the outside of the banister.

"Hi, Daddy."

I'm surprised I even heard him. All I could focus on at the moment were the six feet that separated him from the hardwood floors below.

What would you have done at that moment? Try to honestly gauge your level of anxiety just reading this story. In the comfort of your cozy couch, try to picture your child's beaming face perched precariously close to total disaster. What do you feel? Where do you feel it? In your gut? Between your shoulder blades? Call it anxiety, call it dread, call it nerves.

Whatever you call it, know this: that feeling is real, it is common, and it's actually here to help us. That's right. It's here to help us. No other feeling we experience is able to tell us more about ourselves than this anxiety. Thus, no other feeling is able to call us to personal growth like this anxiety.

Life's relationships seem to be designed this way, inherently producing this feeling. If you think about it, this feeling actually occurs more often and more intensely as we get closer to someone. Rather than provide us the comfort we think we need, close relationships actually increase the probability that we will experience profound pain. Our closest relationships, particularly those under one roof, actually increase the level of anxiety in our lives. Bummer, huh?

Not really. It's not a bummer if we're able to reach a point in our growth where we can choose to experience this anxiety as helpful, and even necessary. Several authors before me have done an excellent job helping people identify the helpful signals anxiety provides for their growth. Rather than allowing our anxiety to provoke us to correct others, what if we took those feelings and looked within ourselves to their source? What does this heightened anxiety tell us about ourselves?

————
Whenever we give in to our anxiety, we create the very outcome we're hoping to avoid.
————

It doesn't necessarily mean you're a worrywart, a nervous wreck, or in need of heavy medication. If we're really listening for the signals, then our anxiety about a loved one speaks of a live, growing passion, a deep concern and care for that person. We would have reason to be concerned if we *didn't* feel anxious watching a loved one making a potentially dangerous decision. Our anxiety, particularly when it comes to our kids, is a testament to how much we care, how much we want great things for them, how much passion we have for life itself.

Whenever we experience this kind of anxiety, it's a call for our own growth. Congratulations! You have entered a customized opportunity designed specifically for your personal growth. You may not have asked for it, and you can always choose *not* to grow through it. Growth is always optional—your choice. You can choose to simply give in to your anxiety instead, but as we discussed earlier, you will pay a price. Remember, emotional reactivity has the uncanny ability of helping to create the very outcome you're hoping to prevent.

But, wait! We've forgotten that there is a little boy dangling from the ledge of the stairs! Let's take a moment to evaluate my options (and we always have options).

> **Growth is always optional— your choice.**

I could have chosen, of course, to do nothing and go on about my business. Giving in to anxiety ("screaming") can take several forms, including running away. Who knows what would have happened if I'd done that. The worst-possible-case scenario would have been that he reached the top, tried to climb over the banister, only to fall backward all the way to the floor. What's the growth potential for me in this scenario? Not much—I would have chosen to avoid it.

My next option was giving in to my anxiety and getting reactive—screaming or lunging or flinching. This would have been understandable, right? My son was in mortal danger and I needed to save him. But think through what might have happened if I'd allowed myself to react like that. I actually could have scared him into falling.

This is the dilemma that faces us every time we interact with our kids. Our children don't have to be in mortal danger in order for us to find ourselves in a growth opportunity. Every interaction with our children, every tiny conversation and every huge argument, carries the potential for everyone's growth. We'll address those interactions throughout this book. But back to the stairs.

So what did I do? By the time this occurred, I had begun presenting the ScreamFree Parenting material publicly, so I felt an extra motivation to remain calm. "Okay, Mr. ScreamFree, what the heck do you do now?" Nothing like having your professional reputation tied to your parenting skills.

So what did I do? I grew up a little. This was not a situation I could escape with any sense of integrity; it was a situation I could embrace for my own growth and my son's benefit. My son needed me to be two things at the same time—calm and connected.

I acknowledged him, "Hey, buddy," without paying too much attention to him. I then gently and slowly moved down the stairs, keeping one eye in front of me and one eye back on him. He kept climbing. I then walked up behind him, stretched up to reach his legs, and gently, but firmly, brought him down to safety, holding him tightly in a loving embrace.

A potential disaster had been avoided. I had somehow discovered a resource within me, a place of calm resolve. I grew. I entered the opportunity, stayed in the opportunity, and grew through the experience.

The Benefits of Growth

Now let's talk about *you*. If you're reading this book, you're probably a frustrated parent. You might be facing so many potential "opportunities" for your growth that you just want to run away. Congratulations! Life hasn't given up on you yet. The very fact you face challenging, even overwhelming situations is a testimony to this. For some reason, the universe and its Creator are interested in your personal growth.

"Blessed are the overwhelmed parents, for they shall receive growth opportunities every day."

But we are the grown-ups, aren't we? By this time in life, shouldn't we be finished growing? Not by a long shot. It's more important now than ever to continue your own growth process, inviting your kids to watch you struggle to learn and grow.

What you want is for your kids to talk with you, share their lives with you. You send mixed signals when you overreact to the information they disclose. If you want your kids to eliminate you as a resource for guidance and support, then by all means, stop growing. Continue to escalate in your reactions and allow your emotions to guide your responses.

However, if you want to be the calm influence, the "cool" parent your children really need, then do everyone a favor and keep growing up.

Why is this so important? As you'll see in the next chapter, if you want to be in charge, you have to be under control. Kids are going to act out the anxiety that exists within their family system. And that system comes fully equipped with an anxiety transfer function. Think of it as auto-playback: if you want to feel calm in your family, that calm starts with you. If you want to invite an anxiety-filled scream-fest, well, that starts with you, too.

As you learned earlier, it's not about them, it's about you.

Reflection Questions

1. What's the hardest part of parenting for you?

   Patience & remaining calm

2. Several have said this: "I was a much better parent before I had kids." How is your view of parenting different now than it was before you had children? How is parenting more challenging? How is it more rewarding?

3. Recall an incident where your reactivity actually made things worse. What could you have done differently? What's a possible different outcome?

4. How much do you consider yourself a grown-up? How has becoming a parent asked you to continue growing?

5. What benefit might it have for your child to see you still striving toward maturity, still seeking your own growth?

Chapter Three

If You're Not under Control, Then You Cannot Be in Charge

Please don't make me angry.
You wouldn't like me when I'm angry.
—Bruce Banner (aka, The Incredible Hulk)

Despite the success of the recent movie a couple of years ago, my favorite adaptation of *The Incredible Hulk* goes back to the campy television show in the 1970s. There's an old Halloween picture of a young, skinny kid, painted green from head to toe that proves my early devotion.

In many ways, the Hulk was the anti-superhero. Bruce Banner may have been the mild-mannered alter ego, but when he got mad, we weren't always sure the green monster was going to act for good. He didn't have a spot on the League of Justice, that's for sure. You might call him one of the original X-Men, a mutant, forever changed by his unfortunate mishap and forever longing to return to normal.

What made the show compelling was the struggle we watched week after week. This nice, peaceful man tried in vain to contain the raging monster lurking just below the surface. We never knew what it was going to take to set him off, but we knew at least once in each show all hell would break loose. Perhaps what was most frustrating for Bruce Banner was that he wasn't fully aware of what the Hulk would do or had done. He was only aware of what he was capable of doing.

That's why the famous quote was so poignant: "Please don't make me angry. You wouldn't like me when I'm angry."

> We continually surrender control over our emotional responses to those around us.

He didn't like him when he was angry.

Bruce Banner could not control the reactive monster within. The control he needed to manage his condition was always in the hands of everyone else. That's why he had to warn the people around him. It was up to them to manage his reactions, because he had lost the ability to control himself. And the results were not pretty. They were usually disastrous.

It's one thing to believe you're the Incredible Hulk when you're seven years old and it's Halloween; that's cute. It's another thing to believe it when you're a grown man having lunch in a public place with your wife and kids; that's sad.

I recently watched a man take his family hostage. He sat there with his wife, his ten-year-old son and a toddler in a high chair. No one talked. The family looked like they had been muzzled, not allowed to make eye contact or interact at all. When the mom started to feed the toddler, I found out why.

After a couple of fussy refusals to open his mouth, the father shouted at the child, "Eat!" There was no pretense of propriety, no understanding that we were all in a public place, an enclosed space. There was only a disrespectful bark.

Later, the older son started blowing bubbles in his drink. This time, the father actually said these words: "You're about to push me past my breaking point!" It's hard to believe a ten-year-old has that much power, that he can push a grown man past his breaking point.

"Don't make me angry. You wouldn't like me when I'm angry."

But the unfortunate truth is many of us live our relationships this way. We continually surrender control over our emotional responses to those around us. When we need them to accept us or validate us by doing whatever we want them to, we make them the caretakers of our emotional remote controls.

Bonzi Wells, a guy who gets paid to play basketball for the NBA, was once fined for making an obscene gesture at a fan.

When questioned later about the incident, he responded, "If that fan was a little more professional, you know, I probably wouldn't have had to do that."

OK, who's getting paid to be there? Who's supposed to be the professional? Please.

Of course, I can't judge him too harshly. We've all been guilty of pinning our emotional responses on others. It started back in the Garden of Eden, with Adam and Eve. After they ate the forbidden fruit, they started the blame game. Adam blames Eve and then he blames God for creating Eve in the first place. Eve then blames the serpent.

Whatever you believe about the story, it demonstrates one solid truth—we've been blaming others from the very beginning.

It's a sign of maturity when you're able to take responsibility for your own actions. To own up to your mistakes without blaming your circumstances, other people, or your childhood—this is when you know you're a grown-up. But that's only one step to bringing yourself "under control."

> **Your emotional responses are up to you. You always have a choice.**

Learning to be "under control" means taking responsibility for your decisions before, during and after you make them. I am not saying you don't ever make mistakes; this isn't about trying to be flawless. This is recognizing that no one, not even your kids, can make you feel anything, think anything, or do anything. Period. Your children cannot push you over the edge, press your magic buttons, or bring you to the brink. They are not that powerful.

Your emotional responses are up to you. You always have a choice.

If You Live by the Remote, You Die by the Remote

You may have seen the commercial where a man is shown watching television, remote control in hand, as his wife enters the room. When he asks what's for dinner, she begins a lengthy monologue on this little dress she's been wanting. The exasperated husband aims the remote at his wife, pushes the fast-forward button and suddenly she speeds up. He keeps the button pressed until he finally hears "Turkey potpie!" The commercial ends with the woman holding the remote. Her husband is sneaking out the back door, golf clubs in hand, when she points the remote at him. She pushes the button to change "his" channel and suddenly, much to his surprise, he puts his clubs down and starts doing laundry.

We laugh at this commercial because it reflects a deep fantasy for us all—getting other people to do what we want, when we want, the way we want. We often cherish the thought of having a magic wand, waving automated commands toward our co-workers, our spouse and, especially, our kids. Wouldn't that be wonderful? Push a button, any button:

"Go to bed without arguing."

"Do your homework."

"Quit hitting your sister."

"Take responsibility for your actions."

"Become a well-adjusted, self-directed adult."

Here's the problem: when it comes to relationships, you can only hold one remote control at a time. When you grab for someone else's remote, you automatically give them access to your own. Don't believe me? What happens when you tell you daughter to pick up after herself and she says no? All she has to do is exert her own choice, a choice not to obey your command and everything changes. Now she has begun pushing your buttons. Now you're locked in a button-pushing contest. Maybe you get louder or more intimidating. Maybe she gets more belligerent, more defiant. Very common. Not very productive.

If you live by the remote, you die by the remote. If you come to rely on your ability to control others, you are destined for frustration and misery. All they have to do is say "no," and you're beside yourself. You're out of control, because you're trying to control something you have no business controlling.

What Does It Mean to Be "In Charge"?

Being in charge as a ScreamFree Parent is a fundamental shift in your objective as a parent. To truly be in charge means having the power to create lasting and continued growth, not just exerting power or demanding obedience. This means inspiring your children to motivate themselves.

Hear me say that again.

To be "in charge" as a parent means inspiring your children to motivate themselves.

This makes for a radical shift, a shift from controlling your kids' behavior to influencing their decisions. Your goal is not to control, but to influence. Remember, you are not responsible *for* your child's responses. You want to continually hold up and respect their ability to make choices, even choices you disagree with. Unless they're free to make their own choices, they can't learn the connection between choices and consequences. We're going to talk more about this later, but for now, focus on the paradigm shift you have to make. You should not be in the business of forcing compliance at all costs. That kind of parenting only works short-term and sows the seeds for long-term disaster. We may not like to hear that, but it's true.

When we try to force our children to comply with our sometimes unreasonable demands, we turn parenting into warfare. We even use warfare terminology: "You've got to pick your battles." I hope we all eliminate that phrase from our rhetoric, because our language has an amazing ability to frame the interaction. Thinking of it as a series of "battles," I cannot help but go into the situation expecting a fight.

In his book *Raising Children You Can Live With*, family therapist Jaime Raser says this: "Parenting is not a series of 'techniques' or 'manipulations' designed to gain control over another human being. It is a special kind of relationship between a parent and a child."

Later, in the same book, Raser says:

> Children can draw parents into interactions that become Us (the children) against Them (authority figures), not Us against the realistic and logical consequences of rules. Us against Them becomes a war. 'Getting tougher' can win battles, but it may also teach that winning is the most important goal and that force and power are the ways to win. Children then learn that, with enough power, they can also win and that this is how the world operates. If they feel they are losing, they simply apply more power.

This battle can seem endless, and that's because it is. There are no victors in relationship battles, just more casualties. When you need your child to comply for your sake, you're creating a power-based exchange that asks them to be the caretakers of your emotional state.

What You're Really Screaming

We've all heard there is more to communication than just words. What comes out of our mouths makes up only a small part of what actually gets communicated. The content of any communication is not nearly as important as the con*text*.

When you scream at your kids, when you get emotionally reactive, you communicate one single message: CALM ME DOWN! No matter what words are actually coming out of your mouth, no matter how long your tirade is, no matter how old your child is, when you scream the message is always the same: CALM ME DOWN! Whenever you react to your child's behavior by screaming, you are actually begging them to help you calm your anxiety.

You are saying you just cannot handle the fact they will not obey or listen or calm down themselves. You cannot handle this, so you flip out.

"I CANNOT BELIEVE YOU DID THIS!"

"WHAT IN THE WORLD WERE YOU THINKING?"

"THIS IS NOT THAT BIG OF A DEAL. YOU CAN GO OUT WITH YOUR FRIENDS TOMORROW!"

Insert whatever words you want; the message is always the same.

"I need you to comply or else I'm going to lose it. And when I lose it, I'm going to need you to comply so I can calm back down. All my emotional responses are up to you."

How is a four-year-old or a fourteen-year-old supposed to deal with that much pressure? And that's what it is, pressure. When you put all your emotional buttons in a child's hands, you become totally focused on them. You have begun a sort of orbit around them, attaching all of your emotional responses to how they perform in school, whether they use good manners, or whatever other choices they're making today. The entire family's emotional life is now tied to the whims, frailties, and growing pains of a child.

"Calm me down, son, because I cannot calm myself."

It doesn't sound much different from Bruce Banner: "Please don't make me angry. You wouldn't like me when I'm angry."

> There are no victors in relationship battles, just more casualties.

So what can you do differently?

You can take back your remote control. You have to make it your number-one priority to hold your own emotional responses in your own hands.

Calming Yourself Down

"That sounds great," you say.

But in the heat of the moment it seems we are more inclined to do exactly the opposite. I know. In the blurry messiness that makes for an anxious moment, we start to rush, we start to panic and we start to focus on the other person. We all have triggers, certain sights, sounds, or words that set us off. Our triggers can vary in intensity, depending on the time of day or the person we're dealing with. No one sets us off quite like our kids.

"I hate you!"

"You're stupid!"

"Mommy, I made an accident in the kitchen."

"She hit me!"

"I wish I had a different daddy."

"I never get to do anything! It's not fair!"

"Why do you always have to go to work?"

"I got my report card today."

"Dad, I just got in a wreck."

"Mom, I think I might be pregnant."

Whoa! That got intense at the end, didn't it? As parenting expert Dr. James Dobson so appropriately titled one of his books, *Parenting Isn't for Cowards.*

Steve Martin has a great scene in *Bringing Down the House.* Upon the advice of his hip and streetwise new friend, Steve's character decides to approach his teenage daughter—who's just stumbled in after an all-nighter—with calm instead of rage. With the facial contortions that only Steve Martin can create, we watch his attempts to stay smiling, cool, and calm on the outside while clearly doing a white-knuckled boil-over on the inside. The results are even better than he expected.

After his daughter told him things that happened at the party, more shocking than he really wanted to know, she was so happy he didn't blow up, she threw her arms around his neck and exclaimed, "Oh, Daddy! I'm so happy to be able to talk to you! There is so much more that I want to tell you!"

Of course, that's just a movie and things don't happen like that in real life, right?

Wrong. I've seen that type of connection hundreds of times, especially with teenagers, once parents learned to control their reactions.

But let's take the same scene and play it differently, this time without the self-control.

Let's say Martin's character reacts more like, well, like any of us might if we weren't working hard at it. What do you think would happen if a daughter came in after being out all night and the father had neither desire nor capability to calm his reactivity?

I'm going to take a leap and say he would lose complete control of himself and hit the ceiling! Given that reaction, how much closer do you think the two would become by the end of that screaming match? What would happen to that father's ability to influence the situation? Where would his authority go at that point? Out the window, just like his daughter would if he kept reacting that way.

Remember, giving into your reactivity actually helps create the very outcomes you're trying to avoid. This is because of a process called anxiety transfer. We've just looked at two different reactions to an identical situation. In the first scene, the father calmed himself down and the result was his daughter became calmer—calm enough to trust him and confide in him. She reacted to his calming influence and the result was a more trusting relationship.

In the second scene we imagined the father allowing his anxiety to get the better of him. He blew up and hit the ceiling. His anxiety over an inability to control his daughter and his fear for her safety then got transferred over to her. Her reaction, therefore, became defensive. A screaming match ensued. And the result was the further crippling of the relationship.

Now many of you might be saying she deserved whatever she got because she committed such a horrible offense, staying out all night! I am not saying that choices to break the rules need go undisciplined. I am not saying that in order to foster a calm and trusting relationship, you need to let your kids go without discipline. Nothing could be further from the truth.

But for you to exercise a position of authority in your family, for you to have the lasting influence upon your child's choices you so desperately crave, you first have to calm down. You have to calm your own anxiety, refusing to transfer it over to your child and make any situation worse.

In order to be in charge, you have to bring yourself under control.

Reflection Questions

1. What situation with your child seems to make you the most reactive?

2. When do you feel the most anxious and get the most reactive? What is your typical way of "screaming"?

3. When you lose your temper, who are you usually tempted to blame?

4. Has anyone ever tried to make you lose your temper on purpose? How did you respond?

5. Recall a time when you were proud of the fact you remained calm and connected during a heated situation. How did your calm presence affect the outcome?

Storytime

This first story illustrates the amazing power of taking the focus off of your kids and placing it squarely on yourself.

Julieanne knew she had to change something. After another screaming match with her thirteen-year-old daughter, Annie, she realized this was not simply a series of isolated fights, this was the dominant form of all her interactions with her daughter. As a single parent, she felt stretched so thin all the time that her resources seemed depleted.

This was going nowhere.

However, instead of seeking help from outside the family, she would constantly ask her children for the kind of support they simply weren't equipped to provide. Without focusing on herself, she would get trapped in the relational dynamic of needing her children to comply for her sake. This was not working. Those relationships were not only worn out, they were deteriorating.

It was at that point Julieanne came to see me and she began working on herself. It was good to finally bare her soul to another adult who would be able to listen, help her identify her own patterns, and even hold her accountable to the new home life she so desired. As she grew, Julieanne began to realize she needed ongoing adult peer support. She started to lean on a pastor at her church. He told her she could call him the next time she felt scared she would say something regrettable. Julieanne was learning to focus less on her daughter, recognizing the more she focused on herself instead, the more she found herself able to be calm and connected at the same time.

But as relationships change, the natural anxiety increases. While Julieanne was shifting her focus and improving her ability to remain calm, Annie kept testing Mom's newfound growth.

Annie wanted to go away for the weekend with some girlfriends. One of the other girl's parents was going to pay for the trip and they were to stay at a hotel, just for fun.

Julieanne's radar went off when she realized the girls were only going to be "dropped off" for the weekend, with no adult supervision. She told Annie no. This set off an intense scene, to say the least.

Annie erupted with more intensity than ever before and Julieanne's newfound calm was put to the test. In the midst of Annie's horrendous screaming fit ("You never let me do anything!" "You're so unfair!" "I hate you!"), Julieanne turned her back on her daughter and went into her own bedroom. Sometimes, we need a break in order to remain calm. She closed the door behind her, shutting Annie out. In tears, this exasperated mom immediately went to the phone and called her pastor. It was eleven o'clock, but she was at her wit's end. The pastor didn't mind at all. But her daughter did.

Annie barged in screaming, "Oh, who're you calling? Someone to listen to you complain about me? That's just great!"

And then she stormed out of the room.

But Julieanne did not acquiesce to her daughter's reaction. Instead, she began talking to her pastor about herself. She did not complain even once about Annie.

"I'm angry," she said on the phone, "and I'm tempted to say things I don't mean."

She told him she was tired and not very good at taking care of herself, especially with all the demands of single parenthood.

"I'm angry at myself most of all."

Julieanne was doing a great job of maintaining her focus on herself. They talked for several minutes and Julieanne's voice began to calm down with each sentence. Simply talking about her own emotions was helping her take the focus off her daughter. Choosing to examine herself was taking the fire out of her belly and allowing her deepest desires for her relationship with her daughter to come to the surface.

As Julieanne's peace began to defeat the anxiety, she noticed Annie's face peering from around the cracked door. Her daughter had been listening at the door the entire time. After she stormed out of the room, she had come back and put her ear at the crack of the door opening. When Julieanne noticed and looked back, Annie quickly pulled the door closed to conceal her eavesdropping.

After the phone conversation was over and Julieanne felt confidently calm, she exited her room and headed down the hall to her daughter's. When she got there the lights were out and Annie was in bed. Julieanne decided to leave well enough alone until the next day.

That morning was a completely different scene. Her daughter did not come down and magnanimously apologize, but she did calmly say she understood Mom's point of view. She had obviously focused on herself that night as well, because she was then able to articulate what was really bothering her.

"I understand you're just trying to do what's best for me, Mom. I really do. I just feel like you never want me to grow up."

Julieanne was able to listen with calm and connection. She was able to hear her daughter's views and express her own concerns about the weekend excursion. The conversation ended with a hug and a tear. Evidently, Annie's eavesdropping ears heard quite a bit the night before. She heard her mom wasn't trying to control her and what she was doing, but Mom was trying to control herself. Julieanne's short dialogue with her pastor spoke volumes to Annie.

She didn't need a heated speech from her mom, she needed a mom committed to focusing on herself, growing herself up, and calming herself down. And that's what Julieanne was beginning to give her.

Annie didn't go away that weekend. On her own request, she went shopping with Mom instead.

Section Two

Keeping Your Cool Means Creating *Space*

When they were very small I suppose I thought
someday they would become who they were because
of what I'd done. Now I suspect they simply grew
into their true selves because they demanded in a
thousand ways that I back off and let them be.
—Anna Quindlen, "Goodbye, Dr. Spock"

You've come a long way so far. In the first section, you learned
that in order to have the best relationships with your kids you need
to focus on yourself, grow yourself up, and calm yourself down.
Now we shift a bit.

As you become a calming authority, your influence begins to
shift. Instead of shaping your family system with your anxiety, creating the kind of relationships you're hoping to avoid, you begin to
influence with the *absence* of your anxiety. Your calm presence

empowers you to become more available as an inspiration to your child, which engenders profound levels of trust and influence.

So what do you do with this growing calm and this newfound level of authority? You continue with what brought you here—you focus on yourself and your responsibility to your children. What we're going to look at in the next two sections is creating and maintaining an environment that facilitates the growth of your children. And, as you know by now, the greatest factor in your child's growth process is your own continued growth as a parent. So it makes sense to shape your environment in a way that helps you remain both calm and connected.

And that means it's time to talk about boundaries.

Many authors and relationship experts have recently been banging the drum for a better understanding of boundaries. In fact, the concept has become commonplace; the word itself has been added to the common vocabulary. But when a relationship concept like this becomes popular, it is easy to get confused about what it really means.

I'm not going to say that boundaries are a simple concept, but I will try to give as simple a definition as possible. Here goes: Your boundaries refer to your *space* and your *place*. Space and place—easy to remember, right? Your space is the emotional and physical territory you occupy in the world. Your place is the fence around your space, the limits of your freedom as it bumps up against other people's space.

And that's it: Boundaries are about your space and your place.

The section you are about to read focuses on creating space. We all need our space—space to breathe our own air, space to grow, and space to discover ourselves. In this space, we get to know our preferences, our temptations, and our tendencies. In this space we learn about our strengths and weaknesses, we learn about spirituality and the faith journey, and we learn about our needs and our wants. In short, it is within our space that we develop our sense of self, our sense of individuality.

As parents, it is our responsibility to our children to create and maintain a family environment that encourages and honors this space, for each person in the family.

The next four chapters will show you that choosing to keep your cool, choosing to be ScreamFree, is the best way to create and maintain this healthy space.

And more importantly, creating space is the best way to help you to remain ScreamFree.

Chapter Four

Begin with the End in Mind, but Let Go of the Final Results

After seeing my newborn son for the first time,
I now know for a fact that I'm on my way out.
His very existence means one thing:
he's here to replace me.
—Jerry Seinfeld

Life does not begin at the moment of conception
or the moment of birth. It begins when the kids
leave home and the dog dies.
—Unknown

Years before *Bringing Down the House,* Steve Martin played his first struggling father character in the movie *Parenthood.* In the film, Martin does a remarkable job showing the roller coaster of emotions we tie to our children's behaviors. He also shows the pitfalls of taking too much responsibility for how they turn out.

61

After he has an especially effective moment with his struggling son, he begins to daydream about his son's college graduation ceremony. As the son delivers his valedictorian speech, he thanks "the most important and influential person" in his life, his father. An elderly Steve Martin stands up to the crowd's applause and his son goes on to recall a moment in his childhood when he was having a rough time.

"But thanks to my dad," he recalls, "I am now the most outstanding, the most confident, and the most well-adjusted person in this world."

A little later in the movie, Steve Martin's son has a major meltdown and again, Dad fantasizes about his overestimated responsibility. In this daydream/nightmare, the scene is chaos on a college campus. In a recreation of Charles Whitman's 1966 University of Texas massacre, we see Martin's son perched on top of the tallest building on campus, shooting his rifle at random victims. The police give a megaphone to Martin, hoping the father can talk the son down. Instead, Steve Martin is completely befuddled, trying to coax his son with pop-psych techniques.

"Good shot, son!" he yells after another successful kill. With a shrug, he explains to bystanders, "It's important to be supportive."

The Paradox of Parenting

We all have fantasies about how our children will turn out. We think about their college choices and career possibilities and we wonder when they might start a family of their own. Some of us even think about our own lives then, traveling to visit our grown children and spoiling our own precious grandkids. These fantasies are precious and usually occur during those wonderful moments when we feel great about our relationships with each child.

At other moments, however, our fantasies also become nightmares. We get fearful about all the potential traps out there and we dread that our child may not have what it takes to make it out in the world. Usually these fear-filled moments occur when our relationship with our child is not going well, when all we feel is the frustration of seeing her make the same mistake again and again.

Like Steve Martin's character in *Parenthood*, we have each vacillated between fantasies of success and failure, depending upon how we're feeling at the moment. And, like Martin, we're not exactly sure how to estimate our influence. What we know we face is a paradox.

> So we have a paradox. Parents shape their children. Children shape themselves. Both are true.

On the one hand, we know parents are the most powerful influence in the lives of children and, thus, parents play the most important role on the planet in terms of shaping the future of humanity.

On the other hand, we know parents cannot be held totally responsible for the choices of their children, for that would lead to an endless search to blame someone else. No child can ever hold their parents responsible for their own choices without sacrificing the very individuality they crave.

So we have a paradox. Parents shape their children. Children shape themselves. Both are true. My answer to this paradox is not to eliminate it, but rather embrace it by changing one small preposition.

We are not responsible *for* our children; we are responsible *to* them.

We examined this earlier in the first chapter. As we begin this new section, looking at the type of environment you want to create in your home, we need to revisit the issue. As you learned earlier, having a responsibility *for* your kids necessarily orbits your life around your kids, needing them to perform so you know you've done a good job as a parent. It also necessitates a technique-driven approach to your parenting; employing whatever behavioral program you can to ensure they turn out as well as you need them to. This does not make for ScreamFree Parenting. This make for anxiety-driven, relationship-damaging parenting.

But all of this does not mean you turn a blind eye or deaf ear to the outcomes you'd like to help bring about for your kids. I would never advocate a passive, "sit back and hope for the best" style of parenting. No, you are responsible to your children for whatever you do to help them make it in the world. So, it's vitally important to take a more intentional look at the type of results you're looking to accomplish. And this means you need to take a serious look at the lasting relationships you would like to have with each of your children.

Beginning With the End in Mind . . .

I've borrowed the title of this chapter from Stephen Covey. "Begin with the End in Mind" is the second of *The Seven Habits of Highly Effective People*, Covey's landmark book on human potential. In that second chapter, Covey leads the reader through an imagination exercise. He asks us to picture our funeral, down to the last detail, especially the attendees. We are to specifically imagine who we would like to eulogize us and what they would have to say. By imaging what we would love others to say about us then, we can see our deepest priorities and principles now. Thus we can organize our present life around those principles, bringing into effect the results we have already imagined in our minds.

That's how the exercise works. And it can be tremendously helpful. What we're going to do here in this chapter is very similar. I'm going to lead you in an exercise to visualize the type of adult you want each of your children to become and the type of relationship you would like to enjoy with each of them. Most importantly, you will begin to see the type of growth you would like for yourself.

Begin by relocating yourself to a quiet place, isolated from the noise and clutter of kids, spouses, housework, and television. Now begin to visualize your youngest child at the age of twenty-five. What year is it? How old would that make each of your other children? How old does that make you? After you've done all the math, allow yourself to get really imaginative. I want you to think about each of your children and ponder your ideal for the questions below. Allow yourself to truly long for this ideal, how you would love it to be, in each of these areas.

- Is your child married? For how long?
- How would you rate their marriage?
- Do they have children? How would you rate your child as a parent?
- Do they have a college degree? A master's? What was their major? What do they do for work?
- How much money do they make? Do they work for a large corporation or do they have an entrepreneurial vision?

These might be the most important questions:

- What is the content of their character?
- What do their friends and spouses say about them? Their bosses and co-workers?
- How self-sufficient are they? What is their decision-making process?
- How well do they take responsibility for their choices?
- Are they physically healthy and active? How well do they take care of their bodies?
- What are your grown children's deepest values? How do they contribute to society?
- How do they carry themselves around others?
- How do they spend their alone time?
- What are their spiritual beliefs and how do those beliefs shape their worldview?

Now the tough part. Recall again how old you'll be at that time. Start to imagine your future.

- Are you married? How do you rate your marriage?
- How healthy are you physically? How well do you take care of your body?
- Where do you live? Are you still working or have you retired? How do you spend your days?
- How have you grown and matured?

Now focus on your relationship with your kids.

- How often do you see your grown children? What type of relationship do you have with them? Are you close? Distant? At each other's throats? Too close for comfort?
- How much respect do you and your children have for each other as individuals? Are you still waiting for one of your children to grow up?
- Do you still support them financially? Do any of them still live under your roof? Do you live under one of theirs?
- How would you rate yourself as a grandparent?
- Are your grown children inspired by you, your success and your maturity? How do they talk about you to their spouses, their friends, their children?

Congratulations. To whatever extent you were able to put some serious thought to those future questions, you have every reason to be proud of yourself. Why? Because while we may occasionally fantasize about it, hardly any of us allow ourselves to truly think forward like that. We are so quick to put off such future imagination as nothing more than irresponsible, wishful thinking. And yet, these are often reflective of the deepest desires of our hearts.

I love C. S. Lewis's thought on the matter. When criticized for urging readers to concentrate on their deepest longings for the future, Lewis came back with this retort. He said not to think of it as wishful thinking, but rather "thoughtful wishing."

And that's what you've just done. What's amazing about the process is the more we engage in thoughtful wishing, the more we find ourselves drawn to actions today that have the best chance of producing those results tomorrow.

That's what it means to begin with the end in mind. By intentionally focusing on the outcome we desire for tomorrow, we encourage ourselves to take the most effective actions today. So, to what end are you working? What goals do you have for this entire parenting exercise?

By taking you through the exercise above, I led you to reflect upon a future when your child is an adult. And that is the entire goal of parenting—to produce another adult.

Like Jerry Seinfeld said, it is our child's job to eventually replace us. And that's the paradox. It's our job to both train them for the job and get out of the way as they learn to do it. Which means, like the old saying, we can lead a horse to water, but we cannot make it drink. So we have to practice . . .

Letting Go of the Final Results

So much of the business world is based on getting desired results. Managers are fired because they did not produce the desired results on the bottom line. Sales brochures and commercials do nothing but promote the guaranteed results. We want to know if we apply this product in the correct manner, we will definitely see the promised results. That's why so many parenting books promise what we want to hear. Apply this program and you will definitely see more obedient, cooperative, and loving children! We guarantee this technique will result in the behavioral changes you so desire. "What works for Fido will work for your child!"

Fortunately, life doesn't work that way.

Children are not machines or pets and parents are neither their operators nor their owners. When it comes to relationships, we cannot ever guarantee or control that end we desire. While working toward that end, we must let go of the need to achieve it. That's the paradox we mentioned earlier. And this is frustrating.

"You mean even though I want my child to turn out to be a loving, responsible adult, I can't focus on turning my child into a loving, responsible adult?"

Exactly. Here's why.

The more I focus on the results I desire, the less chance my child has of authentically choosing that result for herself. The more it becomes my goal, the less room she has to discover her own goal.

I speak a lot to churches and religious groups. One of the primary concerns of any faith community is training their children to love and honor God. For most people of faith, that is the number one goal of their parenting. Thus, they are a little put off when I assert that this is actually not their most important goal. I assert again and again that launching their children into a self-directed adulthood is far more important.

Why? Because if your child is not a self-directed adult, then whatever faith she does develop will not truly be her own. She cannot authentically choose to follow God if she cannot choose, on her own, to follow God. Such a faith would be a borrowed faith at best, one that is still seeking to appease or please others. Again, this brings up the paradox for parents. If I want to make sure my child follows God, then I have to let go of my *need* to make sure my child follows God. I need to create a space for my child to discover God on his own. Does that mean I do nothing? Of course not.

Again, begin with the end in mind. Lead the horse to water . . . We are training them to ultimately become responsible for themselves and no one else. The ultimate goal of parenting is to launch our child into an adulthood where they are self-directed, decisive, and responsible people.

Think about it. What is the number one complaint of parents, particularly those with teenagers? Their children do not take responsibility for their own actions. It is no coincidence, therefore, that the number one hope of parents is that their children become adults who are able to do just that, take responsibility for their actions. This means they are self-directed. That may not be a term you're familiar with, so here are the attributes of a self-directed adult:

What goals do you have for your parenting?

- He knows and pursues what he wants in life.
- She gladly seeks counsel from others, but ultimately makes up her own mind.
- He demonstrates integrity, a demonstrated consistency of his beliefs, words, and actions.
- She holds people accountable for their actions (including her parents), but does not blame others for her own problems.
- He does not let others blame him for their problems.
- She gladly and quickly takes responsibility for her decisions.
- He welcomes criticism as feedback, but does not automatically accept it as truth.
- She takes care of herself in order to be available to others without needing them to take care of her.

Aren't these the very attributes you hope for your children? Aren't these the qualities you want them to demonstrate, the qualities that give them the best chance of success in this world? So what environment do you need to create in your home that can best lead them to develop those qualities? Here's the crux: If you want your children to become self-directed adults, you have to face the truth that you cannot do it for them. In truth, the more you try to *make* them into self-directed adults, the less chance they have of becoming such adults.

... And We Start by Focusing on Ourselves

So what's the answer? Continuing to focus on ourselves. If we want to produce a self-directed adult, we have to first become one ourselves. Especially in relationship to our children. This means creating space for them to make decisions and calming our anxiety about those decisions. This means teaching them the principles of life and then letting them decide whether to accept them and follow them, or fight against them and suffer the consequences.

I often refer to Jesus' teaching style as an amazing model. Perhaps more than any teacher in the history of the world, Jesus displayed a deep desire that people believe in him. And yet, he never wanted to *make* them do it. If he was truly God himself in the flesh as he claimed, then he certainly had the power to make anyone do anything! But he still would not do it, because he knew *a coerced disciple is not really a disciple at all.* He can lead someone to "the water of life" by letting him know the truth about the world. And he can lead someone to this water by sharing with that person the benefits of a life of faith. He can lead someone by modeling the truth himself. But no one can force anyone to drink without compromising that person's ability to choose.

Launching Our Kids into Adulthood

Back when I taught high school seniors, I had the opportunity to witness parents who were able to let go of the final results and parents who were not. For those unable, that senior year was a nightmare. As the idea of leaving for college became closer to reality, the anxiety level of the whole family system shot right through the roof.

In response to that increasing anxiety, some parents gave in to it, beginning to micromanage every aspect of their child's life. They would hover over every homework assignment, tighten the leash on social activities, and constantly check up on the college application process. And it saddened me to watch as their relationships with their children deteriorated.

Other parents would respond to this stress differently. They looked upon this senior year as one step closer to liftoff and thus used it as a chance to hand more and more direction over to their child. This wasn't easy, to be sure, and these parents struggled as they watched their child make decisions. But these parents stuck to their principle of calming their own anxiety instead of asking their child to calm it for them. During the college application process, they would hand over the forms to their son and let him know they were there to help if he needed any. These parents would actually extend their daughter's curfew a little later for that senior year, giving both themselves and their child a taste of what it would be like the following year, when dorm life most likely wouldn't come with a curfew at all.

In truth, these senior year experiences for all these families were not unexpected, given the parent/child relationships up to that point.

On the one hand, for those parents who had always dreaded thinking about the future launching, who had always needed their child to perform for their sake and who chose not to pursue their child's self-direction, that senior year was a logical extension of what had come before. They encountered the enormous battle of trying to rein their child in while the child strained desperately to get more and more "freedom." By the time senior year came around, neither parent nor child was anywhere near ready for the launching process to begin and both would just blame the other for all the problems it created. Thankfully, a number of those families sought help from me and others, and parents and child alike were able to develop the courage to look at themselves and choose to calm down and grow up.

> If you want your children to become self-directed adults, you have to face the truth that you cannot do it for them.

For those parents who had always been training their child for self-direction, however, that senior year went much more smoothly. These were the parents who had progressively extended the freedom and responsibility of their growing child, knowing that was the best way to train them for liftoff. It was still an anxious time, for sure. But it was an excited anxiety, full of planning and dreaming. It was also an experience of trial and error, as both parents and child struggled through the ramifications of increased self-direction. But regardless of the mistakes made, these parents had committed to the principle of beginning with the end in mind and letting go of the final results.

You can, too.

Reflection Questions

1. What was it like for you to imagine you and your family's future? What was the hardest part? What did you like thinking about the most?

2. When you think about your effect upon your child's future, what is your first feeling? Excitement, hope, fear, guilt, dread?

3. If you can be honest with yourself, how much do you hope your children fulfill your own ambitions? How well do you know *their* ambitions?

4. How self-directed are each of your children now? What steps have they taken recently toward self-direction and how have you encouraged that growth?

5. What does it mean to you to "let go of the final results"? What might that look like in terms of your relationships with your children?

Chapter Five

Kids Need Their Room

The children who do best are the ones
least essential to our own salvation.
—Edwin H. Friedman, *Friedman's Fables*

What children need most are parents who do not need them.
What children need most is for their parents to be the first ones
who see them as individuals in their own right, with their own
lives and decisions and futures. Children were not put on this
earth to make us parents feel loved, warm, respected, or appreci-
ated. They were put here to become themselves by becoming
self-directed adults. And they need for us to create enough space to
do just that.

Now before this sounds too much like the permissive parenting of the sixties or some cold and aloof method of detachment,
let's remember what we've said about *space*. Your space is your terri-

tory. It's your freedom *and* your responsibility to occupy a certain territory in the universe. At its most basic, this means the physical space your body occupies. Your body occupies a space that cannot be occupied by anyone or anything else. Now, in America, most bodies take up more than their fair share of space, but that's a topic for another book (look for *ScreamFree Weight Loss* sometime in the future).

But a person's space doesn't stop with just her body.

Your space extends beyond your body to your "personal space," like the distance you like to maintain in a crowded airport. It also, just as importantly, includes your emotional freedom to explore different feelings, ranging from anger to sadness to confusion. Space includes our inner space for self-reflection, self-definition, and self-understanding. Privacy, opinion, attitude, thought—all find their home in our space.

> Everyone has a space to call their own.

In defining the word "kingdom," Dallas Willard, professor of philosophy at the University of Southern California, writes:

> Every last one of us has a "kingdom"—or a "queendom," or a "government"—a realm that is uniquely our own, where our choice determines what happens . . . Our "kingdom" is simply the range of our effective will. Whatever we genuinely have say over is in our kingdom.

In other words, everyone has a space we can call our own. In that space, we have the freedom to explore, to discover possibilities and potential, to make mistakes and learn from them. In that space we can be comfortable and learn to struggle through our discomfort. We don't have to put on a mask or pretend. We can be ourselves with no fear or shame.

Every person ever created, including each of your children, was designed to have a space like this. It's part of why we don't like being told what to do. It's why we learn in our earliest years to say things like, "You're not the boss of me!"

Most two-year-old children have a favorite word: NO! Why is it their favorite word? It's not because they're necessarily rebellious and it's not because they're absolutely depraved little criminals. A two-year-old's favorite word is NO! because she's learning to develop her sense of her own space. In fact, the sense of having some measure of control over things is a vital factor in both mental and physical health.

I remember watching my daughter when she was two, learning to separate herself from us.

On one occasion she looked straight at me, held her arms out as if to push me away, and said, "Don't follow me!"

And then she ran into her room by herself.

A few minutes later she came back out (checking to see that I was still there) and said again, "Don't come after me into my room!"

She again ran into her room for a few minutes of alone time. I could have chosen to take this personally, getting reactive to the idea she didn't want to play with me anymore. I could have also taken this fearfully, getting reactive to the idea she's too young be alone, that she might hurt herself. But what was really going on?

My daughter was developing a sense of her own space. She wanted to play by herself to see if she could. She ran out to see me again because she wanted to know I was still there.

I've chosen the word "room" in this chapter title because it conveys both the physical and emotional space our kids need to fully become themselves. Just listen to our language. "Room" not only refers to a physical location, as in "Don't follow me into my room." It also relates to a sense of freedom, as in "room to grow" and "breathing room." I've also chosen the word "room" because it refers to a literal battleground in most American homes, the child's messy room, which actually provides an amazing growth opportunity for both parent and child.

Kids need their room because without adequate space to explore, experiment and yes, make their own decisions, they can never fully become the self-directed adults we want them to be. This does not mean each child needs his or her own literal room in the house (only a small percentage of the world's families would financially allow for that).

I am talking about the principle of granting each of your children his or her own kingdom, which includes physical space (their bodies, their privacy while in the bathroom, a small corner or a whole room) and emotional space. Without space to learn their own likes and dislikes, without space to make their own mistakes, our kids continue to live a borrowed life and it leaves them with but two choices—fight against everyone's efforts to determine their life (the rebellious child) or simply defer to everyone around them (the passive, robotic child).

Space Out

You've probably figured out by now that creating space means creating some separation. But families aren't supposed to be separated, right?

On more than one occasion I've received a strong objection to this part of the material. During several ScreamFree Parenting seminars, people have stood up and protested that theirs was "not a closed-door family." They strongly argued there should not be any distance within the family, that privacy and respect for each other's space is not a high priority.

> **Without space to make their own mistakes, our kids live only borrowed lives.**

"We don't close doors in this family."

Going back to our goal of launching our children into self-direction, my question back to these objecting parents is always the same: "Until when?" At what point will you recognize your child's right to privacy, to their own space? When they're old enough to drive? When they leave the house? When they get married? If we're beginning with the end in mind, then why not teach this model of respect in the single most influential environment your children will ever know? Why not model now the respect we want them to exhibit later, respect both for themselves and for others?

Don't you want your daughter to respect herself enough to ward off boys and their efforts to cajole her into premature sexual activity? Then you model how she deserves to be treated by respecting her privacy, her own space, starting tonight. Teach her that her space is respect-worthy *now*. Do this not by the words "You should respect yourself," but by the respect you offer to her first. Encourage her to close her door. Knock when you want to enter. Ask her if she wants to talk about her feelings and respect her answer. Buy her a diary and promise that, no matter what, you will never, ever read it. And then don't even ask if she's ever used it.

Since coming out of the womb, our children have been on a journey to separate from us. Even their need to bond closely at the beginning is for the express purpose of developing a sense of personal security without us later. As we learned last chapter, they need to separate from us to become what we all want them to be—adults. So now, when they are close to us, we can be the ones to help introduce healthy separation.

By voluntarily creating more space for our children, we remove their anxious need to separate with drugs, premature sex, gangs, or suicide. Kids do not need more of our anxious reactivity about these choices—they need more emotional space from us to learn to respect their own individuality. Hard as it may be for us to hear, it is far better for our children to make bad choices on their own than to have them run to those choices as an escape from our anxiety.

Our non-anxious creation of space actually makes those bad choices far less likely. Calming ourselves down communicates so much so powerfully to our children, namely that 1) their separation from us is more than okay, it is good; and 2) our respect for them is growing, not lessening, as they get older and their choices take on more significance.

Calling It Theirs, but Still Treating It Like Yours

But, as hard as this might be to put into practice, parents cannot determine how children use their space any more than children should be able to determine how adults use theirs. It is *their* space. It's not a privilege; it's a right. It's part of being human. Every man, woman, and child has a kingdom.

This means you cannot tell anyone else, particularly your children, how to feel. Parenting experts Scott Turansky and Joanne Miller tell a story about a mother whose four-year-old daughter sometimes gets into grumpy moods. This mother decided to take on her daughter's emotions as a challenge. She held her daughter, tickled her daughter or made cookies with her daughter. Sometimes this "worked," but other times her daughter would just continue being grumpy.

Eventually, the mother told her daughter, "It looks like you want to be sad for a while, so there's probably not much I can do about it. Let me know when you're feeling better."

Turansky and Miller conclude the story by saying, "This mom recognized that she could do a number of things to help, but ultimately the decision to change was up to her daughter."

But we don't just want to make sure they feel good. Often we want to know our children feel regret or remorse after they've misbehaved. We think we need to change our children's hearts before we can release them out into the world. It makes us feel better if we know they *feel* the right way.

But it's not your job to change the hearts of your children, telling them how to think or feel. By trying to do something you aren't meant to do, you invade their space and violate their rights as people. And since this effort is led by your anxiety, you inevitably end up creating the very type of rebellious heart you were hoping to change in the first place.

The beautiful irony is that learning to respect their feelings (and their right to feel them) actually increases the chances that they will feel the way you hope they do.

Similar to respecting this emotional space, you cannot give them a room (or any physical space in the home, even a small corner), call it theirs, and then continue to act as if it belongs to you. If it is "their" room, then it is up to them to keep, explore, clean (or not clean), and organize. That means no barging in. Knock. And ask if you may come in. Wait for them to invite you in. I know it seems weird; their room is in your house, after all. But this is what it means to extend respect for another person's space. You'd like them to give you the same respect, right? But you cannot expect that respect when you don't initiate and model it toward your child.

The Power of Keeping Your Cool

This is a difficult principle because it demands you confront your own anxiety. Give them space? What if she starts to hide stuff from me? What if she starts to make some bad decisions? What if she hurts herself? What if she feels abandoned? What if she has to struggle? What if, what if, what if?

What is always behind our invasion of their space is, of course, our own anxious reactivity. We cannot let them struggle for too long because we need them to do it, whatever it is, quickly. We cannot let them feel bad or have a really grumpy day because that reflects on their life, which we view as our responsibility. If they are not happy then it must be because of something I have done or failed to do. We get reactive about their mess because we think they are becoming a slob and we cannot let that happen because that would go against everything our parents taught us and on and on and on.

We are so afraid of giving our kids their room because we fear what they might do with it. We might "give them enough rope to hang themselves." I understand this fear and I share it with you. And yes, there are certainly age-appropriate degrees of separation and space.

> What is always behind our invasion of their space is, of course, our own anxious reactivity.

But becoming a ScreamFree parent is about learning to operate out of respect for your highest principles, not in reaction to your deepest fears. You can never operate out of your fear because you will, as we learned in Section One, inevitably create the very outcome you fear. The importance of giving your children increasing space as they age is far greater than the fear of what they might do with that space. It has to be or you will constantly feel forced to shift your focus back upon your kids, feel responsible *for* them, re-enter the orbit around them, and so on.

The remarkable power of creating room for your children is you get to be amazed by what they do with it! As you reduce your anxiety about their choices, their choices begin to astound you. I know you might doubt that, because you can so accurately predict your child's responses. But I want you to listen in on this recent exchange between a coaching client and her eight-year-old daughter.

Mom was starting to respect her daughter's "room" and her daughter didn't know what to do.

Daughter: Mommy, I know I have to clean my room tonight, but I'm just too tired!

Mother: Why do you have to clean your room, honey?

Daughter: Because you guys always make me!

Mother: Honey, you don't have to clean your room if you don't want to. It's your room.

Daughter: What? Since when?

Mother: Since I decided that it is your room.

Daughter: But it's going to take a long time to clean it!

Mother: Honey, you don't have to clean it.

Daughter: I don't?

Mother: No, not if you don't want to. But let me ask you something. Do you want it clean?

Daughter: Well, I like to know where everything is.

Mother: Then clean it. I'll even help if you want me to.

Daughter: But it'll take too long and I'm tired!

Mother: Then don't clean it.

[My client then started to walk away.]

Daughter: But Mommy?!?

Mother: Yes, honey?

Daughter: I guess I could do a little tonight and then finish it tomorrow. It's not like I have to finish it tonight or anything.

Mother: That sounds like a great idea. Let me know if you want any help.

Two days later, her room was not spotless. But it was picked up and it was more organized than most other days. And the little girl was ridiculously proud of herself.

I think Mommy had every reason to be proud of herself as well.

Contrast that with the battles most parents get into with their children. It has nothing to do with your child being a slob or you being a neat freak. The battle over the messy room has nothing to do with cleanliness! It also has nothing to do with the child's disrespect or ingratitude. The battle over the messy room is a battle over space. When we choose to call it "their" room, but then continue to act like it belongs to us, we invade our child's space and eliminate the possibility that they can develop their own sense of respect for their own space.

But when we extend the type of respect for their space we want for our own, then watch out. You'll be amazed at what happens. The question is, can you calm yourself down enough to truly create space?

I believe you can.

Eight Ways to Create Space for Your Children

When you are ready to start calming your own anxiety and creating more space for your children here are some practical ways to do that. These are NOT techniques to get your children to behave, but rather practices for you to begin with the end in mind, yet let go of the final results.

1. Respect their space and privacy. Starting as soon as you can calm your anxiety about letting them close the door, make it a practice to always ask or knock before entering their room (or if they're in the bathroom) and wait to hear their response. If they say "no," then tell them you'll come back later and ask again.

2. Calm your anxiety about their messy room. If it is "their" room, then let them keep it the way they want to. Tell them that twice a year, for biological reasons, the entire house is going to be thoroughly cleansed and that includes their room. In between those times, let their room be theirs. Whenever you feel anxious about their mess, go clean your own room. Of course, you can let them know what you think of their cleaning practices, and you can decline their invitation into their lair for your genuine fear of tripping over all the junk. But leave it at that.

3. Respect their choices. Give your child an allowance appropriate for her age and then let her spend it any way she chooses. Even if you can only afford a single cent, it is the principle that counts. Go ahead and teach her about different options (investing, spending, and giving), but don't expect her to take care of her money any better than you do. When we give our children money, we give up the right to determine how that money is used. It isn't really theirs if we're going to tell them how to spend it. If you want your money spent in a certain way, then go ahead and spend it that way. It's yours to begin with! But once you give it away, you give it away.

If we want kids to learn, value, and become decisive about money, then we have to allow it to become truly theirs.

4. Calm your anxiety by giving up your need to know how they feel. Most of the time, they simply do not know (the same is true for most adults). Your anxious need for them to know just makes it more difficult. Paradoxically, the less you *need* to know, the more they end up telling you.

> The power of creating room for your kids is that you get to be amazed by what they do with it.

This doesn't mean neglect any concern about their feelings—this is about being calm *and* connected at the same time. So inquire about their feelings, show interest in helping them learn to express themselves. But let go of your need to make sure they feel the "right" way, which is nothing more than the way you think they should feel and is usually about your anxiety related to your own feelings.

5. Similarly, give up your need to know "why." Asking any child, from toddler to teenager, to account for his motivation at the time of his mistake is a fruitless exercise. He simply does not know most of the time. And your need to know is much more about you than it is about him. But you want to know he can demonstrate some form of reasoning. You think this eases your fears about their chances out in the world and how that might reflect on you.

But here's the irony: if he did know and he was able to carefully explain his well-thought out reasoning for hitting his little brother or skipping school, your fears wouldn't be eased, they'd be justified! If your son could intellectually recall his reasoning behind his choice to neglect his homework and then lie about it, you wouldn't be less scared, you'd be more fearful than ever!

"Before I feared, in my most anxious moments, that he might be a delinquent. Now I know for sure!"

Either way, asking why has no fruitful end. At the very least, it puts the child on the defensive because you're asking him to give just that, a defense.

6. Let them struggle. Always answering your child's questions, or constantly telling your child what to do to solve a problem, is denying that child the chance to develop his own skills of discovery and innovation. "Mom, I can't do this!" has an uncanny ability to stir up our anxious need to fix the problem.

But if you rush to answer, then you deny them the space needed to figure things out for themselves.

Letting them struggle might look like this: "You can't? Man, that stinks. What have you tried so far?"

After their response, ask them, "So what are you going to do about it?" The more you can calm your anxiety while watching them struggle, the more you'll be amazed at their growth (and yours).

7. Allow your kids to disagree with you and learn to respect their arguments. This is incredibly difficult for anxious parents, but allowing (and even encouraging) your child to disagree with you creates a profound mutual respect in the parent-child relationship.

Questions like, "This is what I think, what do you think?" show a remarkable respect for your child as a separate individual.

As you become more and more ScreamFree, you can actually learn to learn from your child, choosing not to "yes, but" your child's every point, but actually validating their thought process and their importance in the relationship.

8. Rarely look your kids in the eye when talking with them. I know this sounds absurd and even heretical. Eye-to-eye conversations are incredibly intimate, however, and bring about high levels of vulnerability. Thus, these types of conversations lend themselves to patterns of intimidation and defensiveness. Yes, there are times, sweet and nurturing as well as stern and serious, when it is very helpful to address eye to eye. But these times are rare. Use them sparingly.

If your goal is to allow your child to explore her space and share that process with you, then engage in a common activity that takes your eyes off of each other while keeping you con-nected. Go on a walk or a drive, build Lego projects, play a game, skip rocks, throw the baseball, go shopping, whatever. Not only does this common activity disarm you both from a defensive or aggressive posture, it also, most importantly, gives you the ade-quate space to remain calm, yet connected.

And if you haven't guessed by now, that's the main point about giving your child space—it makes it easier for you to remain ScreamFree. Becoming ScreamFree helps you create space; and creating space helps you become ScreamFree. Beautiful, isn't it? And believe it or not, you're already on your way.

Reflection Questions

1. How much privacy do your children have a right to?

2. What's the hardest part about extending more and more space to your child?

3. Has your child ever marked anything—a book or a door—as "Private, Keep Out"? Have they ever pulled away from you when you've tried to embrace or kiss them? What has been your reaction?

4. What are your deepest fears about extending your child too much space?

5. How much freedom does your child have to hate you? Disagree with you? Express anger toward you and your decisions?

Chapter Six

Resistance Is Futile;
Practice Judo Parenting

Resistance is futile.
—The Borg, *Star Trek*

I have found the best way to give advice
to your children is to find out what they want
and then advise them to do it.
—Harry S. Truman

No, I am not a *Star Trek* geek. I actually make fun of my friends who are. But I do like one of the villainous enemies from the show. They are called The Borg. They are a race of cyborgs, and they all belong to one collective consciousness (my geek friends had to help me craft this sentence). What that means is they each have separate bodies, but no thought processes or will of their own. For The Borg, there is no such thing as

95

individuality. When they capture others, they "assimilate" them into their collective being. They erase any individuality of the captured. From what you've read so far, you can see that they do the exact opposite of creating space—they eliminate it. They are so powerful in this purpose of assimilation that they simply utter one mantra: "Resistance is futile." Regardless of your efforts, you will eventually be assimilated.

Unfortunately, The Borg's way of operating is similar to a parenting model that many of us grew up with, and even more unfortunately, many of us continue to practice today. You've heard it before, maybe even out of your own mouth, "You have a rebellious streak and you and it's my job to break you of it and mold you into x, y, or z." This is ultimately parenting by assimilation, whereby parents *need* to exercise their power to bring all the children into line in order to feel in control of the family.

In my therapy and coaching practice, I see this type of family system all the time. And whenever I see this type of arrangement in a family, I know one thing for sure: the parents feel threatened. The parents are unsure about their position of influence, and they feel intimidated by the child's exertion of will. So, the parents step up their use of power to counter the child's. Here's where many familiar "power struggles" occur. When a child does not show an act of willfulness, then the parents assume she is fine, and so they do not feel threatened. Thus they do not need to exert themselves. What this leads to is a relationship mainly based on power struggles with little room for connection off the battlefield.

Far too often, the only way the parents connect to their children is to bring them into the fold whenever they challenge the status quo. If there is no challenge, then the parents' anxiety gets reduced and things remain relatively calm. If there is no challenge, however, there is no connection. That's the real tragedy here. As a child in this family, you are either the rebellious one in need of constant attention or the "lost child," the one "we never have to worry about." Both of those options will create a difficult journey for your child (and you) in the years ahead.

ScreamFree Parenting offers a different way. Ironically, it employs the same phrase The Borg uses: "resistance is futile." The difference is that instead of saying it to our kids, we say it to ourselves.

Throwing Down the Gauntlet

As mentioned before, when children exert their will, most parents view it as a direct challenge to their authority. How many times have we heard this well-meaning phrase in parenting magazines and radio talk shows: "When children challenge you, you've got to pick your battles."

Listen to the language we use! This assumes that the exchange between you and your child will be a hostile one in which there is a triumphant victor and a vanquished foe. This type of rhetoric assumes that the challenge issued by your child is just that—a challenge. I'd like to offer up instead a different word and a radically different idea. Instead of considering your next trying interaction with your child as an impending Waterloo, consider this: in your child's developing growth, he is constantly *testing* you. In doing so, he is not plotting an invasion or laying an ambush. He, instead, is testing you to see if you can be trusted. He is testing you so that he can see that you are dependable, stable, and consistent. And trust me, he desperately needs you to pass.

You might be thinking, "You mean when kids 'push our buttons' they aren't really wanting us to give in?"

Yes and no. Yes, their anxiety wants you to cave at that moment, but their "inner adult" is begging you to not get ruffled and remain calmly focused on yourself.

I know, this testing so often feels like a fight. It feels as if your kids are digging a trench and loading their bazookas. What they are really doing, however, is throwing down a gauntlet. In medieval times, the gauntlet was a protective glove of sorts worn by knights and the like. When thrown down on the ground at the feet of an adversary, the gauntlet was an invitation to battle. Picking up the gauntlet was an acceptance of the invitation, an acceptance of the mutual responsibility for whatever happens next. And the same is true in parenting. When kids throw down a gauntlet, they are testing you to see if you are willing to take responsibility *for* them.

> Your child is testing you to see that you are stable and consistent. And he wants you to pass.

There are such a wide variety of gauntlets that children throw down: "I'm bored," "Are we there yet?" "You're not fair!" "I don't want to do it and I'm not going to . . . ," "I hate you!" Can you recall what the pit of your stomach felt like the last time Junior uttered one of these phrases? Many parents find themselves reaching down, snatching the gauntlet, and engaging their child in an all-out battle before they know it.

So, what does this have to do with The Borg? By employing the phrase "Resistance is Futile" when considering a child's emotional show of force, a ScreamFree parent can instead use that child's own momentum to change the encounter completely.

Let me explain by mixing metaphors a bit. The practice of judo, or "The Way of Gentleness," is a discipline whereby the momentum of the opponent, rather than raw, brute force, is used to change the outcome of the encounter. It is a model of conflict, if you will, that chooses not to pick up the gauntlet. In a conflict, the student of judo is still engaged with the other person, choosing to remain connected. But the participant is not going to attack the other, or accept his/her invitation to fight. The judo participant is, instead, going to accept the other's momentum as belonging to the other, and something not to be resisted. Instead, it is to be respected. Just listen to the words of Jigoro Kano, the father of judo:

> . . . If one enters a contest with the sole idea of not being defeated, automatically, the body becomes stiff and defensive—and they appear to be entirely preoccupied with the idea of winning their contest, without any sign of aspiring to higher accomplishment. [Instead], the principle is to evade the opponent's strength or change one's position to reduce the effect of the strength applied.

Jigoro Kano often spoke of the willow tree. He observed that in the harsh winters of Japan, seemingly stronger trees were losing their branches to the heavy snow while the supple willow tree simply allowed the snow to glide off of its branches. The willow uses the weight of the snow and bends with it rather than attempting to overpower it. What this approach to conflict necessitates is a willingness to learn the other; a willingness to carefully observe the *other* and his/her momentum. Only then can you know how to respond without directly resisting their invitation to combat.

You can already see the parallels between the judo model of combat and the ScreamFree model of relationships. Your children, through their own anxious efforts to handle their emotions and responsibilities, will try to engage you in a test. Think of the two-year-old deliberately picking up a forbidden object, immediately after you told him not to, while looking devilishly at you the entire time. Think of the school-age girl screaming that you're the worst mommy in the world because you won't let her do "what everybody else" does. Think of the teenager; enough said. These are all tests, tests that only become "battles" when we take responsibility for our child and pick up the gauntlet.

Refusing to Pick Up the Gauntlet

But ScreamFree Parenting offers another way altogether. Remember, judo is the art of going with another's momentum. So the ScreamFree parent asks, "How can I employ my child's desires for motivation, connection, and discipline? How can I bend like the willow tree when they throw gauntlets at my feet?" Let's explore the ScreamFree possibilities with some common "tests."

"I'm bored."

This is the classic gauntlet. And we so often are quick to pick it up. First, we get angry. "Bored? How could you be bored? Why don't you go play upstairs with all of those toys I bought you?" Then, we get anxious. "You mean you can't find anything to do?" We might even think to ourselves, "Is this kid totally uncreative? What have I done wrong?" Finally, we overcompensate. "Look, you could go outside and find Jimmy, or you could go upstairs, or you could do this, or you could do this, blah, blah, blah."

A ScreamFree response could choose, instead, to never pick up the gauntlet in the first place. "Wow, you're bored? That stinks. I hate it when I'm bored. What are you going to do about it?" No resistance, just go with the momentum and actually join right alongside your child as she faces her *own* dilemma.

Your children, through their own anxious efforts to handle their emotions, will try to engage you in battle.

"Are we there yet?"

Another classic. You've been in the car less than ten minutes, and the echoes from the backseat have already started. And you've got another two hours to go! What is the typical, anxiety-driven response? To pick up the gauntlet, of course. "No, we've got an hour to go, so just sit tight and be patient." Now the battle has commenced. "A whole hour?!? I'm never gonna make it! You never said it would take that long. How long is an hour anyway? I'm so bored already."

A ScreamFree response could choose, instead, to never pick up the gauntlet in the first place. "Wow, you're already asking that question? You must really not want to be in the car today." Empathy. "Come to think of it, I don't want to be in the car either. And I don't want to be in the car for a whole hour either. I think I want to be out of the car more than you do! What do you think?" Joining alongside your child, you can then commiserate together (and actually have a fun time doing it).

"Mommy, I can't do my homework."

A woman called me wanting to come to one of my seminars. Her objection wasn't the time, or the location, or even the price. Her objection was about what to do with her children. I told her we had babysitting available. "No, that's not it. You see, I need to make sure my husband can make sure our daughter does her homework." That's the type of statement a parent makes when anxiety is driving the boat.

You can imagine our conversation after the seminar. She picked up on the irony. "So Hal," she said, "If I understand correctly, I was saying 'I don't know if I can come to a seminar to focus on my parenting, because that would mean taking my focus off my child. And if I have to take my focus off my child, then I need my husband to do it for me.'" I loved what she said next: "But you know what? The times in the past when I just couldn't be there to watch over her homework, she's done just fine."

Homework hovering is a major epidemic around the world. It serves as a wonderful microcosm of everything we're talking about in this book. The homework hoverer is saying, "I'm responsible for you, Son, so I need to make sure you do all the work you're supposed to do. And since you cannot do anything else until it gets done, then I can't get anything else done either. So we're going to work on this together, making sure you get it done, and get it done right." What is difficult for the hoverer to see is that the very act of hovering makes the problem worse. The child's motivation is now completely confused because it's now about keeping Mom or Dad sane, easing their anxiety.

The child's unconscious thought becomes, "So the thing between me and getting to play with my friends is not really the homework, it's Mom's anxiety. Well, that stinks because when Mom gets anxious it becomes more difficult to concentrate, more difficult to stay focused, and more difficult to think my own thoughts."

You cannot orbit around your child without giving her the distinct impression that the world revolves around her. With the homework hovering, you forget whose homework it really is. As you learn to calm your own anxiety about her performance, then you do not have to pick up this gauntlet. "So, you've got a tough one there, huh? I hate it when I can't figure something out. What are you going to do about it? Who can you call in your class that could help you?"

> A ScreamFree Parent never picks up the gauntlet in the first place.

Our child's homework is *supposed* to make them struggle. It is *designed* to be difficult for them. That's the whole point! Calm yourself down and let them struggle. Let them invite you alongside to help them through the struggle, but do not try to "be there for them." You can't. It's their problem, not yours.

"I hate you!"

Allow yourself to feel this one. What emotional reactions come to the surface? What do you immediately want to say?

"Well, I certainly love you, young lady."

Or, "How dare you say that to me after all I've done for you!"

Years ago, I had a coaching client whose seventeen-year-old son, in a spiteful effort to communicate his anger and hatred towards her, decided not to open any of his Christmas presents from his parents. Not one present. For a full year afterwards, they sat, unopened, in an upstairs closet. Now that is a pretty big gauntlet. Mom was so tempted to pick it up by reacting emotionally. She felt so much pain she wanted to throw him out of the house, lash out at him every day, tear up his things, you name it.

> You cannot orbit around your child without giving her the impression the world revolves around her.

She decided to focus on herself instead, asking herself some incredibly tough questions about her relationship with her son. "What's been going on that would lead us to this? What would lead a kid to act so spitefully, even denying himself material gifts just to get back at his parents? Is he just a psychopath, or have I been contributing to the pattern this whole time?"

With this pause, Mom could then ask herself the best question of all. "What can I do differently to begin repairing this relationship? And how can I do it without losing my cool, getting reactive, and simply making things worse?"

What's great about the ScreamFree path is that the second you want to get on it, you're already there. What I mean by that in this case is that whatever decisions she decided to make with her son, from there on out, had the potential for positive change, simply because she would be acting out of self-awareness and self-direction. By simply stepping back and choosing not to react, she assured herself that her next step would not be reactive. And then she could choose her next step, rather than having it chosen automatically by the previous patterns of combat.

"I don't wanna do it, and I'm not gonna do it."

Ah, the sound of metal hitting the floor. Even as I write this, I want to pick up *this* gauntlet. "Oh yes, you are, young man. You're going to start showing some respect around here. I'm sick and tired of hearing you say what you will and will not do. You don't make the rules around here, mister, and it's time you started accepting that fact." If you haven't said it, you've definitely thought it, right? I have.

A ScreamFree parent could choose another response. Choosing to focus on herself, the ScreamFree parent could pause and ask herself why this demonstration of will bothers her so much. "Why do I take it personally when he asserts his will? Do I feel threatened? Is he out of my control? How far is he going to take this? Am I raising the next Hitler?"

The irony is, of course, that the more we do take it personally, the more reactive we get to this demonstration of will, the more we encourage it. Emotional reactivity simply creates more emotional reactivity.

But again, the entire goal of parenting is to launch our children into the world as self-directed adults. We want them to be capable of asserting their desires, making their own choices, and taking responsibility for their actions. We want them to be able to stand up for themselves and choose for themselves what they will and will not do. We just don't like it when they practice demonstrating that will on us.

"Sure, I want him to say "no" to his buddies when they want him to try smoking pot, but I sure don't want that attitude with me when I tell him to come inside."

Our goal is not to stifle their expressions of will, desire, and emotion. Our goal is to help steer those expressions along the most productive paths. As you learn to keep your cool, you can see this defiant stance as yet another gauntlet, and you can choose not to pick it up. "You're not going to come inside, huh? I guess you really don't want to, because you usually don't talk like that to me. I'm going to let you think about that for a few minutes."

> Your goal is not to stifle their emotions but rather steer them toward productive expression.

After a few minutes, you return to offer him a choice. He can come inside or face a consequence. And it's totally his choice.

Why *Should* Our Children Obey Us?

What this forces us to do is ask ourselves a very tough question. Why *should* our children obey us? What in the world is their motivation? Is it to please us? How long do you want that? Not very. What we want is for them to do it for themselves. We get scared when we don't see them operating with their own motivation. "They should do it just because it's the right thing to do!" Right?

So why in the world should my son obey me? Because I said so? Because he should respect my authority? Because he needs to learn to obey his elders? Yes, yes, and yes, from my perspective. But that's not *his* perspective. Why, from *his* perspective, should he obey? What's in it for him? What is his motivation for coming inside, or going to school on time, or turning in his homework? Why should he do any of this?

As long as the only answer I can give to this question is from my perspective, then I am simply inviting a losing power struggle. Period. As long as I can only answer what I think his motivation should be, and that motivation is "because it's the right thing to do," then I am really saying that his motivation should be the same as my own. And I *need* him to obey because I don't know what to do if he won't. I don't know how to relate to someone who doesn't automatically want to do the right thing, or doesn't want to please me. But that sounds like "responsible *for*" thinking, and we now know where that takes us.

So, in order to adopt the "responsible *to*" model instead, we need to start asking ourselves some more questions. What motivates our children? What do they really want? What *questions* can I ask that will help them discover and explore those desires instead of picking up their gauntlets and going head-to-head?

This takes changing your thought patterns, I know. This can be tough stuff initially. And I'm not promising you that it will eliminate conflict in your home. But part of changing your thinking should include the way you think about conflict in the first place. Consider one last quote from Dr. Kano:

> Before and after engaging in a match, opponents bow to each other. Bowing is an expression of gratitude and respect. In effect, you are thanking your opponent for giving you the opportunity to improve your technique.

Be the first to bow to your children. Not out of deference, but out of respect and gratitude. Hopefully one day, they will bow in return, but even if they don't, you will have grown. And that's what ScreamFree Parenting is all about.

I leave you with a letter I received from a parent of three, ages four, two, and three months. Listen to her as she comes to understand the value of practicing judo parenting.

Dear Hal,

I'm writing to thank you for your help with my four-year-old. She is going through a bout of negativity and frustration lately that I haven't been able to find a cure for. The other day, we wasted more than an hour of our day when she broke down trying to write the number two. She traced it and then looked up pouting and said, "Mommy, I want to write a two, but I can't do it."

"Would you like me to make dots that you can trace?"

"No."

"Would you like me to help your hand write it?"

"No."

"Is there another way you want me to help you?"

"Tell me how to do it."

"Okay. Put your pen on the paper right here and . . ."

"No! I KNOW I CAN'T DO IT!" she screamed and then broke down in tears. I was so frustrated.

Eventually, her tears turned into angry screams (which aren't allowed in our house), so I sent her to her room, all the time wondering if I was making the right choice (and feeling like a really mean mom). I wanted to hold her and tell her it would be okay, but nothing I did was making it better. And sending to her room just angered her more. The crying eventually stopped, and the number two was forgotten, but the day never really got better.

Then I read about your "Judo Parenting" concept. That's why I'm writing—to tell you what happened today.

Here we went again. My daughter wanted to play on the computer, and I told her she could after she changed out of her pajamas and into some regular clothes (it was noon). She went to her room and laid out the clothes she wanted to wear while I finished up on the computer. A few minutes later, she walked in and said, "Mommy, I can't get my clothes on."

Me: "Why, honey?"

"I just can't get my tights on."

"Do you want me to help you?" (We were about to reenact our "number two" day.)

"No!"

So then I remembered about the gauntlet and the idea of non-resistance. "Okay, honey. Let me know if there's anything I can do for you."

"But Mommy, I really can't get them on."

"Okay, honey."

"But Mommy . . ." She started to cry and walked to her room on her own. A minute later, she cried a little louder. But then two minutes after that (I was watching the clock on my computer), the crying stopped and I heard her call me from her room.

"Mommy, I think I figured out how to do it."

"Did you figure that out by yourself?" I asked, walking into her room.

"I did!" She was BEAMING. I couldn't believe it. It's later today, and she is sitting on her bed reading a book. She is much happier than yesterday, and so is her mom.

Thank you for your suggestions.

Jill T., Alpharetta, GA.

Reflection Questions

1. Reflect for a moment on your childhood. How did your parents respond when you tested them? What could they have done worse in response? What could they have done better?

2. We've all repeated the mantra: "You've got to pick your battles." This is because so often it feels like we're in a war, trying to get our kids to do what we want them to do. What's a more productive, more principled way for you to think about it?

3. What does is it look like when your kids test you? How reactive do you typically become?

4. How might your family change when you stop resisting your children and start going with their momentum?

Chapter Seven

You are Not a Prophet
(and Neither is Grandma)

Language exerts hidden power,
like a moon on the tides.
—Rita Mae Brown

There's something wrong if you're always right.
—Arnold H. Glasgow

This is a chapter about language. No, not about reducing the
use of curse words around your children (although that would
probably be wise). This is about the power of your language to
shape your world and the worlds of each of your children.

Remember watching your children as infants, wondering what
was rattling through their heads? I remember questioning what my
baby's thoughts could be. Since she had no words to attach to
those thoughts, did she think in pictures or sound? I remember

watching the process of her learning those first words; those first sentences then appeared seemingly out of nowhere. The next time you get frustrated because your children don't listen to you, think of this: how do children learn to speak with an accent? Kids are actually fantastic listeners from the very day they enter this world. They have keen ears with which to hear every syllable, every inflection, every tonality in our interactions.

It doesn't take long before they begin to articulate phrases that surprise us, utter thoughts that astound us, and repeat sentences that embarrass us. A coaching client of mine, Cindy, learned this the hard way.

When her daughter was three years old, Cindy took her on a walk through the park. It was there Cindy learned how well her daughter had been listening to one of her often-repeated phrases. And of course, this happened at a ridiculously inappropriate time. It always does.

The phrase was, "You must eat your vegetables or you'll get scurvy."

This anxiety-based threat was something Cindy told her daughter repeatedly, even embellishing it with a horrifying picture of what rickets can actually do (not that she really knew, but she painted a pretty horrible picture anyway).

Well, that day as they were walking through the park, Cindy and her daughter encountered three people walking toward them. One of the three had an unfortunate physical ailment that disallowed him from walking normally. As they passed on the sidewalk, Cindy nodded a polite greeting and kept walking. Her three-year-old daughter, however, had something to say.

She stopped in her tracks, turned around, put her hands on her hips, and proclaimed indignantly, "He should have eaten his vegetables!"

Almost every parent has a similar story, some even more embarrassing. What this story illustrates is another way we shape the relational environment of our home—our use of language. Linguistic experts have been extremely helpful in teaching us how remarkably powerful we are as parents in shaping the very thought patterns of our children. Language is the currency of all relationships, including how any of us relate to the world outside of ourselves. It gives us vocabulary to express thought, grammar to govern our interactions, and stories to shape our worldview.

You are probably aware of all this. You've probably read or heard material about the language transmission process that has blown your mind. What you may not be aware of is how the words you use around and about your children actually shape their sense of space.

Like we've seen in the previous three chapters, keeping our cool helps create and honor our children's *space*, their freedom to grow into self-direction. By placing limits on our own freedom, we thereby create and honor theirs. When it comes to our language, especially the words we use about our children, we again need to limit our freedom. We simply do too much talking about them. Too much comparison. Too much categorization. Too much prognostication. And it's time to stop.

Becoming a ScreamFree parent means taking a very hard look at our own anxiety-driven need to label our child's tendencies and predict our child's destiny. Before you think you may not have this problem, keep reading. Let's begin by looking at the power of labels.

The Power of Labels

All of us can recall countless stories of the power of labels. They can be innocently applied and yet become insidiously powerful. The truth is, labels are among the most powerful forces that shape our relationship with the world. Labels have the remarkable ability to stick far beyond their reasonable lifespan. I'm sure you've heard about two adult daughters still thinking about themselves as "the pretty one" and "the smart one." With two sons, it's usually more like "the athletic one" and "the smart one." These labels affect us all. Each of us could list several that hang on us like the stickiest Post-It notes.

Take a moment now to glance at just a few of the labels parents commonly use. Which ones have you been carrying around all these years?

A gifted child. Full of potential. Funny. An underachiever. A little slow. Lazy. High maintenance. Laid-back. A strong-willed child. Beautiful. Melodramatic. The one we never have to worry about. A bit of a troublemaker. Skinny. Big-boned. A hard worker. The star. The black sheep.

Now, not all of these sound damaging, I know, but trust me, they can be. Did you see yours? If not, try to think about it for a second. Now, say it out loud. Think for a minute how much this label has shaped your opinion of yourself. How has this shaped your decision-making? Your career choice? Your mate selection? How does this label still affect you today?

Here's the tricky part about all of this. Often these labels seem accurate; they don't simply arrive out of thin air! Labels are typically based on some observable trait or behavioral pattern. All labels are based on some measure of demonstrated truth. One year, Johnny, despite his demonstrated intelligence, did poorly in school. So, he'll always be "an underachiever." When she was seven, Suzy blew up in anger on a regular basis, so she forever has "a temper problem."

But hear this: *you are not a prophet.* Most likely, you are also not a biogeneticist either. You cannot adequately predict how your children will turn out based on your own or your family's physical, mental, and emotional characteristics.

"You know, he gets his temper from his daddy."

What?! How do you know that? What does that even mean?

"You know, she's gonna be a neat freak just like Mom was."

What?! Why would you pronounce such a curse? Just because at one time your child demonstrated a certain pattern of behavior does not

> **Labels are among the most powerful forces that shape our relationship with the world.**

warrant them being branded with a label for life. And just because someone else, like an aunt, a teacher or a coach, slapped a label on them does not necessarily make it TRUTH. We are so quick to judge our children according to small slices of life, without ever seeing a broader picture of the different possibilities.

I love the quote by noted poet, photographer, and legal guru Gerry Spence, "I would rather have a mind opened by wonder than one closed by belief." Especially the belief of someone like an anxious parent.

Whenever we label our children, even in innocent recognition of certain characteristics, we severely limit their space. We risk creating a permanent handicap to their future development. We stamp out the wonder inherent in the childhood journey. But labels are not the only way of creating such a handicap and deflating the curiosity in a child.

The Magic of the Self-Fulfilling Prophecy

I was four and my brother, Jay, was five. It was Christmas at my Granny's house. All the extended family were there. We were playing with our new Legos on the floor when something occurred to our dear Granny. She saw that while I was struggling to stack two blocks together, my brother was busy building the Taj Mahal.

"Boy, Hal's gonna have to make a living with his mind, because he's sure not gonna make one with his hands, like Jay."

Now this was an innocent comment, to be sure. My sweet Granny meant no harm by it and the whole family laughed it off as a cute observation. Except the comment soon took on a life of its own. Sometimes it was retold for its own sake, but most of the time it had a reference. Anytime from there on out, what do you think was said anytime my brother did something creative or constructive with his hands? What do you think was told around the family gathering every time I did something outstanding in school?

"You know, Granny always said that Jay would end up making a living with his hands."

"Well, you know, Granny always said that Hal would end up making a living with his mind."

So, here we are, almost thirty years later. Do I even need to tell you that my brother has worked in several hands-on occupations (chef, vet's assistant)?

As for me, Granny wasn't too far off. I'm a family therapist; I work with other people's minds. Am I saying this is all Granny's doing? Of course not. But there is magic at work here.

All of us can cite one example of a similar story with similar results. It is very difficult to determine how much influence such stories and labels have upon us. But we cannot deny one thing—they are powerful.

> Whenever we label our children, we severely limit their *space*.

Let me say a word here about extended family. It's very important to surround new parents with support, but this can often be a potential minefield of conflict. I once watched a new grandfather with his daughter and her first child, a six-month-old boy. The baby was fussy around feeding time and was not taking to the bottle of formula. The mother was trying several tactics to feed her son without much success.

In disgust, her father barked, "I don't know why you don't just give the kid cow's milk. It worked just fine for you when you were a baby."

The new mother replied it's been known for a while now that infants' stomachs aren't ready for cow's milk until a year old, but her claims to this effect went unnoticed.

"It worked just fine for you, it'll work for this kid."

So let's see. Since this new mother was a baby, we've landed a man on the moon, put a home computer in nearly every home in America, and connected the world through an invisible network of technology, but we've made no advances whatsoever in the nutritional requirements of infants? Here's the difficulty: whenever we choose any method of parenting that differs from how our parents raised us, we risk indicting them and their effectiveness as parents.

Yes, *A ScreamFree Guide to Leaving Mom and Dad* is on its way. And yes, *ScreamFree Grandparenting* is in the works as well.

We love to categorize, compare and contrast. For some reason, it helps parents and our extended families feel as if we know our children. And we love to know our children. After all, what kind of parents would we be if we didn't? We've weathered the storms of the dinner table and the bedtime blues. So, as they venture out into the world, say for a sleepover, we arm the unsuspecting family with a list.

"They're finicky, you know."

This list may include sleeping habits, the order of bedtime rituals and an extensive list of all their favorite foods. When they come home saying all went well and they even ate green beans for dinner, we find ourselves putting them back into place: "But you don't like green beans!" As if their palates are already determined; as if we are the gatekeepers to any new preferences.

Why do we do this? Because in our anxiety, we love to prophesy, to categorize, and to label. It helps us give some structure to our world. It helps us to feel involved, on top of things, and capable of handling whatever unknowns lie around the corner. But what does it do to our children?

Are All Labels Damaging?

Here's a radical idea for you. *What you say about your kids is more important than what you say to them.* Sounds strange, but it's true. In this light, how powerful do even seemingly harmless phrases such as "Daddy's girl" and "Momma's boy" become? Think for a second about the implied meanings behind such phrases. "Daddy's girl"? Really? Does he own her? Will she continue to be "his" when she becomes a teenager, an adult, a parent? When does she become her own? Does she ever? And let's take a look at "Momma's boy." How do you suppose that would affect a boy's sense of self? We may toss these labels around in all innocence and affection, but they hold incredible power in the lives of our families.

> What you say *about* your kids is more important than what you say *to* them.

What about some of the labels we mentioned earlier? Funny. Hardworking. These don't sound like such bad qualities to have. Well, they're not. In fact they are great qualities; they are also horrible labels. Why?

Your child overhears you say, "Megan is such a clown all the time. She's always making us laugh and really livens things up around here."

If Megan hears this enough, what Megan will learn is this: "My job in this family is to make people laugh. Even if I don't feel like it, I have to try my best to be funny. I heard Mom say so herself, I liven up the place."

Try this one on for size: "My Dylan is such a hard worker. When it's chore time, I can always count on him to set the pace for the other kids and show them how things are done."

What happens when Dylan doesn't feel like leading the way? What we do with any repeated label, no matter how positive, is eliminate their freedom to be an evolving, developing human being.

What we must learn as parents is to fight for our child's right to evolve. We must fight for each child's right to create their own uniqueness in the world. What a gift we give to our children by refusing to stunt their personal development by adhering to them some "personality." What a gift we can give by stubbornly refusing to compare them with their siblings and disallowing extended family members to label or categorize them. We give them the gift of discovery.

The first place for this to begin is within ourselves, naturally. Think of how we brace for an explosion at bedtime simply because there have been similar explosions recently. We're already prepping for a battle when this ever-changing child may be in a completely different mood. I know this is incredibly hard, because we are so frustrated, but we must hold on to the truth that with children (like the stock market) past performance is *never* a guarantee of future results!

No one is ever always anything. No one is ever always lazy or ever always smart or ever always defiant. Just because your teenager wanted money the last time she did the dishes does not account for why she's doing the dishes tonight. No good can come out of accusing them. Just because your child struggled in school last year does not necessarily mean he will struggle every year. It is simply not so!

Strategies for Success

Change Your Vocabulary.

This is an incredibly simple change you can make to defend your children from the onslaught of labels. Take the harsh words "always," "never," "all the time," and "constantly" out of your vocabulary for good. Replace them with two more realistic and forgiving ones like "can be." You'll be amazed at the way this changes the very way you think about your child. By saying "can be" instead of "always," you are recognizing the propensity for change. And change is woven into our very nature.

Here's an example. The next time your daughter launches into a monologue about why her life is so unfair, resist the urge to say, "You are always so dramatic!"

Instead, pause.

Take a deep breath and state, "You *can* be really dramatic when you feel like it. It must be really tough to be twelve. I can barely remember myself."

This small change acknowledges the inner thespian in your child, but it does not lock her into a "personality" where she loses her freedom to be different.

Expect Your Kids to Surprise You.

Believe it or not, your kids are constantly searching for new chances to start new patterns. But since relationship patterns always involve other people, it becomes difficult to change the dance without changing dance partners. They cannot choose different parents, so it's up to you to change.

What that demands from us is a continuous, persistent desire to expect them to change, to act out of their best character. This, by no means, calls for some pie-in-the-sky naïveté about their limitations and it does not mean becoming lax in the face of continued behavioral patterns that cause problems. As we discuss thoroughly in the next section, there are consequences for those behaviors and you are called to enforce those consequences with consistency. But you cannot let those patterns determine your feelings toward and beliefs about your child and his/her future. Despite their limitations and mistakes in the past, we must continually fight for their best character to evolve, fight for their right to always, always, change at a moment's notice.

Become an Advocate for Your Child's Evolution.

Your child is a work in progress. His fate is undetermined, his personality yet to be locked in place. Even his looks will consistently change! You have to become a champion for your child's continued evolution. This means refusing to allow extended family members to categorize or label them. This means stubbornly searching for their best traits and choices and singling those out as the clearest indicators of their capabilities.

It means, most of all, constantly checking yourself internally and calming your deepest fears that because of this or that pattern of choices, your child is going to become violent or depressed or ugly or unemployable.

You are their biggest influence and what you think and say about them will shape them more than any other force in the universe.

Champion their evolution and watch them grow.

Leave Your Mom and Dad.

You have children of your own. You live and operate in an adult world. You are more responsible to more people than ever before. You are growing up. That means it's time to launch from the nest. I know, you don't live at home anymore, but that is only a matter of geography. It's been said that the umbilical cord is the most elastic material in the universe. The launching process is the most important journey of your life and it is by no means an easy one. We've already looked at that in Chapter Four.

Your need for Mom and Dad's input should decrease as your adulthood increases.

Now, I know this is a hugely complicated issue and one that will be fully addressed in another ScreamFree book, but put simply, you need to be actively growing your relationship with your parents to a more adult-to-adult dynamic so you can parent your own children without still feeling like a kid yourself.

Know When to Say When.

What we ultimately have to recognize is our desire to understand and categorize our children's behaviors is really a desire for something else altogether. In reality, we want to show ourselves and others to whom our kids really belong. Therein lies the problem. They don't really belong to us. They belong to themselves and to their Creator. When we pigeonhole them into a certain pattern of behavior, we limit their ultimate potential. We limit their discovery. We take from them the one certainty in life: change.

So, learn when to say when. Years ago, we gave our children beautiful names; let's stop there.

Reflection Questions

1. What label did you grow up with? How has that label continued to affect you and your decisions well into adulthood?

2. What labels have you already placed upon each of your children?

3. How might your discussions about your children change if you absolutely refused to hang a label, prophecy, comparison, or curse around their necks?

4. When is the last time each of your children genuinely surprised you with their behavior? How did you react?

5. What would be different if you approached every new interaction with your child without an expectation of their responses?

Storytime

This next story involves a man and his ten-year-old daughter both having to adjust to a terrible situation. Look for Robert's revolutionary decision to create space, calm himself down and become more available to his daughter than ever before.

A client named Robert got divorced shortly after his daughter, Jessica, was born. His relationship with his ex-wife remained terrible and his relationship with his daughter suffered as a result. Suddenly, Robert's ex-wife discovered she had cancer and soon tragically passed away. Jessica was only ten years old and had endured more than her share of suffering. Now she had to move in with her father and his newly blended family. To make things even worse, she had to start at a new school in the middle of the year.

Robert had his hands full already adjusting to a new wife and her children. Now he took on the challenge of embracing his devastated little girl and the mixed emotions he felt over his ex-wife's death. He needed space and he needed to avoid intruding upon Jessica's room. Father and daughter were both facing a difficult challenge to grow.

Jessica was strong, but even youth has its limits. The Friday before Mother's Day, Robert got a call from the school. The class had started to make cards for their mommies, but Jessica just sat quietly crying by herself. By the time Robert got there, she was inconsolable. He himself was gripped by a flood of emotions. He felt so much pain for his daughter.

And yet, to be brutally honest, he felt inconvenienced, even angered by this whole situation. He could have chosen to become bitter and resentful. Instead, he chose to grow.

This is how Robert was able to make one of the greatest parenting choices in history. Who knows where ideas like this come from? It doesn't matter really. What matters is that Robert and Jessica connected that day in a way they'll never forget.

Robert took Jessica out of school for the rest of the day. He called work and told them he'd be back in on Monday. Then the two of them went to Party City. He bought balloons and helium and permanent markers. They went to a nearby park, where Robert slowly explained that just because Mommy died, there was no reason why Jessica couldn't still send her a Mother's Day card. They just needed to make sure the card could make it all the way up to Heaven.

Taking the inflated balloons, he showed Jessica how to write whatever message she wanted Mommy to read. The heartbroken child wrote, "I miss you, Mommy. I love you, Mommy. I can't wait to see you in Heaven."

When she was finished writing, they tried to estimate how long it would take the balloons to reach Heaven. Then Robert set his watch alarm to beep in a few hours.

Robert used that time listening to Jessica, creating a room for her to explore her own feelings. She moved from recalling her favorite memories of Mommy to venting anger at her death and all the changes it brought. This anger included having to adjust to life with Daddy, a new stepmother, and new siblings. All this change was just too much.

Robert could have chosen to become defensive when she spoke ill of his new wife and her children. He could have objected when she talked about how much better it was when she lived with Mommy. Robert chose none of these responses; he chose to simply remain calm and let his daughter explore her space.

Daddy and daughter were in a deep embrace when the watch alarm went off.

"Daddy, did Mommy just get her cards?"

"Yes, honey. She's reading them right now."

Robert wasn't a genius. He was a confused and conflicted man who chose to set his own feelings aside for a moment to help his daughter sort through hers. He was a brave man who recognized his emotional process was not his daughter's business. As awkward as it was, he chose to be responsible to his daughter in that way. And he was able to revolutionize their relationship in the process.

Section Three

Keeping Your Cool Means
Creating a *Place*

There is no such thing as
"fun for the whole family."
—Jerry Seinfeld

A stand-up comedian tells this story about a hot Saturday afternoon. After working all day mowing the lawn, he walked into his house only to find it crawling with kids. He didn't even know some of these little people. It seemed every person under the age of thirteen in the whole neighborhood was in his house.

He was hot. He was tired. He was a little confused. What he needed was a good, hot shower. Not only would that soothe his aching back and shoulders, it would be a great way to get away from the chaos that was loose on the first floor of his house.

Soaked and soaped from head to toe, he could feel the stress and tension leaving his body. But then he heard something: the door to the bathroom swinging open. Next came the unmistakable sound of two six-year-old girls giggling. He was just about to tell them to leave when the shower curtain flew open.

There stood his daughter, pointing her finger toward the middle of his body and educating her friend.

"See!" she explained. "I told you!"

The girls flew out of the bathroom in a flurry of laughter.

Boundaries are both freeing *and* limiting.

Kids need to know their place. Space without place is chaos. You may have been wondering about this as you read the last section. Okay, Hal, enough about space. When are you going to talk about discipline? Structure? Setting limits?

I saw a commercial recently with a woman on the beach, shouting that she wants to be free of the constraints of time, space, and her cell-phone calling plan. SUV commercials suggest that with their latest vehicle, there are "no boundaries." The possibilities are limitless. There is no constraint on what we're capable of. We cherish these fantasies of unrestrained space.

But think about trying to live that way. Imagine the responsibilities that would come with unlimited space. Being omnipresent eliminates one of the longest-running excuses for not getting things done: "I can't be two places at once!"

Just as space refers to our relationship with ourselves, place largely refers to our relationship with others. When your space bumps into someone else's space, you discover your limits; you become a little more aware of your place.

The greatest conflicts in life—in all of human history—are a result of two people (or groups of people) claiming the same space simultaneously. When two kids are in the backseat of a car, they will sometimes draw a line down the center of the vehicle.

"Better not cross over this line. Over here is my space."

And they go to war defending their kingdoms.

Place lets us know where our freedom stops and someone else's freedom begins.

Boundaries are both freeing and limiting. In fact, freedom without limitation would be disastrous. Space without place would be anarchy, no rules, no way to determine right or wrong, no means of discerning good guys from bad guys, no possibility of protection against predators, no way to order life at all. On the other hand, place without space has no allowance for free choice, emotional expression, disagreement, or exploration.

Using a metaphor I will explain in the next chapter, it is your calling as a parent to set the table for your children, ensuring every child has a secure place in the family. This place at the table is a place where each child is accepted as an individual, yet expected to act as a member of the family system.

The truth is you are already setting this table, one way or another, by how you set the emotional tone of the family's interactions. The question is this: Will you set the tone with your anxious reactivity or will you set the tone with your principled decisions?

Chapter Eight

Parents Set the Table by Setting the Tone (and Vice Versa)

Ask your child what he wants for dinner
only if he's buying.
—Fran Lebowitz

My mother's menu consisted of two choices:
take it or leave it.
—Buddy Hackett

If you were to ask a child to describe their ideal home life, you might expect something like this: "getting to do what I want, when I want, for however long I want." Sounds a lot like vacation. Vacation is great, isn't it? Getting up when you want, wearing pajamas until noon, eating Cheetos instead of Cheerios for breakfast. It's a chance to take a break from the mundane and indulge in

137

things. The kids love it. We love it—for about three days. Then we all start to get cranky. We start to get tired of the lack of routine and the abundance of freedom. We start to long for the familiarity of home and the comfort of routine. As adults, we recognize this.

Children, however, lack the wherewithal to understand that watching *SpongeBob* or MTV for five straight hours and feasting on Ding Dongs could actually start to make them miserable.

> Stability and structure are necessary components in a healthy home.

When children are given too little structure in the home, strange things happen. They choose to do what they want, when they want, and then get terribly frustrated when they find themselves unhappy. Parents in this dynamic throw up their hands in disgust thinking, "Why aren't they happy? We're letting them get what they want!"

Here's something to think about: children don't always want what they *say* they want. [Rare is the child who says he wants a nightly dinner with his family and a set bedtime. Even rarer is the child who functions better without those things.]

Stability and structure are necessary components in a healthy home. This chapter is about the parental role of shaping these for each of our kids. We have a responsibility *to* our children, a responsibility to set a place for each of them in the family. Often, we think of this responsibility in a condescending manner, like it's our job to "put children in their place." This type of anxiety-driven emphasis on punishment, even embarrassment, is not what we're talking about here.

It's better to think of it like making sure to set a place for everyone at the dinner table. It is your responsibility to your family to set the table with calm, consistency, and commitment.

This means we're talking about structure.

"Structure?" you say. "What's that?"

Structure probably seems like something that happens in other people's lives. And you're not far from wrong, because believe it or not, there really are people out there who have structure in their lives. That's because these people have a good sense of place. They know where things "fit" in the scheme of things. In their family, it's an understood thing. Each family member has their place and knows what it is. This means clearly defined roles, an actual hierarchy in terms of authority and a clear understanding of what choices are available and what consequences follow those choices.

The Two Sides of Parenting

In his book *Raising Children You Can Live With*, Jaime Rasor teaches us to understand the dual nature of our parenting role. There is a *personal* side to parenting and a *business* side. Under the *personal* heading fall such elements as fun, togetherness, nurturing touch, and play. These exist in special moments that draw us to our knees in gratitude and lift us to our feet with joy. They leave us dying to talk about our kids to anyone who will listen. Ever known a co-worker who seemed to have a new story each day about the cute things his kids were doing? Ever been that co-worker?

The *business* side of parenting isn't nearly as much fun. Under this category fall the basic operations of the family: setting schedules and rules, enforcing consequences, establishing curfews and bedtimes and providing the basics of food, clothing and shelter. And don't forget about supervising schoolwork and teaching how to clean those toilets.

Do children need to know they can have fun with you? Of course! Do children need to know you are the authority in their world? Absolutely. All of these things need to be done in order for the family to function in a healthy way. But *how* it gets done differs from family to family. Commonly, one parent performs the business side, while the other enjoys the personal. One stereotype is that Mom is the nurturer and Dad is the disciplinarian, but it can just as easily be the other way around. Sometimes the roles are not as clear-cut. Maybe Dad is a loving papa to his little girl (who in turn battles constantly with Mom), while demanding perfection from his two boys. Or Mom is best friends with "Sis," her eldest daughter, while tough as nails with her son (usually hoping to train him to be a better man than his daddy).

All of these manifestations are attempts to work out the balance of the business and the personal—a difficult proposition, I know. One of the unavoidable truths about the way families function is this, however: the balance will work itself out somehow. It may not be the most functional balance and it may leave one parent (or sometimes even the oldest child!) having to do all the "dirty work." What is most common is that the lines between the personal and the business get blurred beyond recognition.

This was the struggle of Jim, a divorced father of two teenagers. He so loved the fun times with his kids and he so hated having to set rules and enforce consequences. So, in a very typical pattern, he would plead and plead with his teenagers to comply, all the while showering them with material gifts and lax curfews. When his children inevitably broke the rules, Jim became so infuriated he would explode. "I give them so much and all I want to do is enjoy my time with them! Why can't they just obey me without me having to get upset like this?"

Jim would take it personally that his children broke the rules, and he would react by getting upset. Then, after his reactive explosion, he would feel tremendously guilty. In the end, he would allow this guilt to take him over and he would back off any disciplinary action whatsoever. Of course, completing the cycle, his children would then respect his authority even *less* and continue to disobey even the most lax of rules. In the end, the blurring of the personal and the business led to a disintegration of both, with very little fun and very little structure.

There is a personal side to parenting and a business side.

The ScreamFree Way

What ScreamFree Parenting helps you do is keep these two sides of parenting separate, leading you to develop the balance within yourself, and within each parent. This means you can operate with all the seriousness you need to establish order without sacrificing the joyful times and feelings you really crave.

Here's how it works: As you learn to calm yourself, it is far easier to operate out of your principles. And just as you teach your children, there is a solid principle about work and play. That's right—you cannot play outside until you take care of your chores.

In order to enjoy the personal parenting times with freedom and love, you have to take care of the business side first.

This means stepping up to the plate and asserting yourself as the authority in the family. You set the table, metaphorically, so everyone, including yourself, can enjoy the nice dinner. This means setting your children in their place. Just as you recognize kids need their room, you also claim your right to privacy. You make expectations and rules very clear, in a matter-of-fact way, without any hint of anger or anxiety. Because you're already working hard to give your kids their *space* (as we talked about in Section Two), putting them in their

All patterns, no matter how ingrained, can be changed.

place does not come across as an authoritarian power trip. You are a calm and connected authority, one who does not need compliance in order to feel like the leader, but one who commands respect and expects obedience.

Some parents gravitate all too quickly toward the disciplinarian role, however, as an effort to control the uncontrollable. By exercising their power over those dependent upon them, they can mask their feelings of inadequacy and intimidation. This is not the ScreamFree way to provide structure.

Setting the table means focusing first on yourself and your parts in any and every developing pattern. Think about that for a second. If a behavior is getting replayed over and over again, it becomes very easy to focus on the other person, the one whose behavior you want to change. But here's the trick—a pattern always involves more than one party. And if you're experiencing a pattern with your child, then guess what? Somehow you're contributing to the ongoing behavior.

What helps is focusing on your part of the pattern without faulting yourself or anyone else for the whole problem. It is a pattern, nothing more and nothing less. And all patterns can be changed. Just change one part of the pattern—yours—and the pattern necessarily has to change along with you. So, again, it is profitable to focus on yourself.

Jim, the divorced father of two we looked at above, eventually learned to focus less on his kids' misbehavior and more on his reluctance to set and maintain a clear structure. The more he began to set the structure, the less he found himself taking it personally when his kids chose to disobey. And the less he took it personally, the more they respected him, in time.

So what are some of the barriers to fully accepting and asserting your authority as a parent? What exactly is the anxiety most parents have to address when it comes to accepting and asserting their position of authority?

Friendship Parenting

We love our kids. We love spending time with them, we love having fun with them and we love those wonderful times of personal connection. Because of the intensity of these feelings, it is incredibly tempting to compromise our principles. As a therapist, I see red flags anytime I hear about the "friendship" between parents and kids. This is not so much because of what it does to the kids. (It does plenty of harm, yes, and many others have said so before me).

I see red flags because of what it does to the parent-child relationship. This friendship type relationship is often an effort by parents trying to make up for what they didn't receive from their own parents and what they're not able to receive from themselves.

But what most of these parents are attempting to do is simply love their kids! They love to spend time with them and absolutely cherish those rare close moments of connection and affection. This is almost intoxicating, especially as the children age, because these moments are so irregular and so fleeting. As they get older, those moments do not necessarily become infrequent, but they come with much less predictability. We look for and hold on to those loving moments of kindness, fun, and yes, even friendship.

But, what does this buddy-buddy approach to parenting do to the family? It undermines the parents as they attempt to set the table because they no longer have a position of authority. Once the parents begin looking to the children to fill any sort of emotional need, the children can no longer look to the parents for stability or guidance. In this light, "friendship" parenting is obviously not a healthy model.

Now, you must understand children don't have a firm grasp on where their space ends and yours begins. So, expect them to try to expand their space, enlarge their territory. They won't want to share right away. They'll keep saying "Mine!" like the seagulls in *Finding Nemo*. They'll flip out completely when you need to leave in five minutes and they have just one more level to go before rescuing the princess warrior. They're just fighting for their space, defending their territory, trying to discover the borders of their kingdom.

But, hear me well. I am not saying you should let them run wild or let them act selfishly without any restraint. I'm saying just the opposite. Part of our responsibility is to provide them their own space by setting their place. This means giving them their room and letting it be theirs. It also means letting them know what is most decidedly not theirs. They're not going to like it when you set those limits, but fighting for their space is a normal part of healthy development.

Children have the very difficult task of asking for us to provide structure while striving to claim as much territory as possible. Parents have the very difficult task of setting limits on their child's space while respecting the freedom within those limits. It's tricky, sure, but parenting isn't easy. It's an opportunity for challenging growth.

In their book *The Seven Worst Things Good Parents Do*, John and Linda Friehl shed some light on this topic:

> Children need and desire structure. They don't know how to ask for it directly. In weak systems, they also get seduced by the lack of structure. They get used to it, intoxicated by it, and then they can't let go of the inordinate amount of power they have acquired. The ultimate dilemma for parents and children when it comes to this issue is that they both want to be liked because they love and care about each other and yet they both need structure. It surely isn't the child's job to provide the structure and at some unconscious level, children know this. The result isn't very good.

In other words, kids want parents to give in, but they also want them to hold firm. Think of it this way: parents give instruction. It's what we do. It seems like hundreds of times each day, we tell our kids what to do, when it should be done, and how to do it. Giving instructions is not just something we do—it's something we have to do!

The very word "instruction" comes from the words "in" and "structure." Basically, it means "to put structure into." By giving our children instructions, we are bringing structure into their lives. Sometimes, kids resist our instruction. Unfortunately, too many parents then "scream," either by blowing up or running away; they either repeat their instructions louder or they give up and give in. Why does this happen? Because it is easier than standing on your principles in the face of adversity.

Hierarchy, Ritual and Routine Are Not Bad Words

So much of the cultural revolutions of the last half century have centered on rebelling against hierarchy. Citing the mantra of the sixties, "Never trust anyone over thirty" to the bumper sticker you still see today, "Distrust Authority," groups have sought to revolutionize society by challenging the structural status quo. And some of these challenges can be wonderfully credited with ending segregation and championing the equal rights of women. These challenges were healthy, necessary, and long-overdue corrections to the abuses of hierarchy, especially toward women and minorities.

But some challenges to authority have gone so far as to question the validity of any hierarchy at all. Since hierarchy was so easily abused, the argument goes, then the very structure of top-down authority must be discarded.

But again, this reactive stance throws the baby out with the bath water. Just because authority is easily abused does not warrant discarding authority. The damages of having no authority, especially in the lives of children, are just as horrendous as the damages of abusing authority. What is needed is a nonreactive acceptance of positional authority. What is needed is ScreamFree Leadership, a type of hierarchy that appreciates its role with integrity.

What we are talking about here is balance, the only thing in life that can never be taken to an extreme. When it comes to providing structure for your family, balance is needed, for there are extremes to be avoided.

You can choose to have a structure that is entirely too democratic, with no authority other than the consensus of all the family members. This always ends up as a chaotic mess of anxiety-led claims to unlimited space.

On the other hand, you can choose a structure that is entirely too *auto*cratic, with nothing but extremely rigid, authoritarian rules to be followed or else. This always ends up as a constricting mess of either reluctant compliance or desperate rebellion.

To illustrate, let us return to the idea of setting the dinner table. In the *chaotic* family structure, dinner is always up for grabs. There is no set time for dinner and it is usually catch-as-catch-can. This makes for a seemingly "relaxed" atmosphere, but it is really chaotic because everyone's appetites become out of sync and everyone's timing becomes haphazard. Snack times blend into dinner time and snack foods (those that are easiest to "catch") become dinner fare. What really suffers is family togetherness and harmony, the *personal* side of parenting we looked at earlier in this chapter. I am not saying the family dinner hour is the only time for togetherness and conversation; I am only using the dinner table as an illustration for the overall family structure.

In the overly *rigid* family structure, family dinners are not only mandatory, they are the linchpin of the whole family lifestyle. There is no room for playing a little longer outside in the long days of summer, there is no switching seats at the table, there is never a time to pull out the TV trays and enjoy a family show together. In this scenario, *place* takes so much priority over individual *space* that there is no room for discussion, disagreement or individual preference.

What often happens is a confusing back and forth between chaos and rigidity. The family will go weeks without any routine. Then, when the anxious parent finally has enough, he or she begins to implement this new "from now on" type of rigid schedule. This anxious reaction never inspires anyone to change and leaves the parent feeling exhausted and unappreciated, not to mention hopeless.

I've been a firsthand witness to the sad evolution of many families who allowed their child to be the unquestioned captain of their ship.

Here's an example. Their child hated dinner. Not just what was being served, although she did balk at that, but the act of eating together as a family. When her mother asked her to sit at the table, she blatantly refused. She insisted she was not hungry, yet she would ask for a bedtime snack only thirty minutes after the family finished eating.

By the time this little girl was three years old, she knew exactly how to get her way in all matters, not just those related to family dining. She had a great weapon, you see, and it was her fabulous set of lungs. All she had to do was utter a single piercing note and her family was instantly brought to their knees and she was spared the "agony" of family dinnertime. They came to see me because they felt trapped by her tantrums.

And they were trapped. But not by her tantrums. They were trapped by their anxiety. I listened as the mother spoke of her outbursts.

"She just won't come to the dinner table! We've about given up."

I asked, "What's the worst thing that could happen if Mandy doesn't get her way?"

Immediately, she replied, "We'd never hear the end of it. She would rant and rave until we finally gave in and let her watch TV instead. I just don't think I could take such a scene."

"So, you're telling me that the worst thing that could happen would be that a child would throw a fit for a few minutes?"

"Well, you don't understand. She can really scream. She once yelled so loudly that she was hoarse for three days!"

Before I could say another word, the father interjected, "Wait, is that really so bad? Is that really worse than what we are teaching her by constantly giving in to her demands to avoid dinner? I mean, we can handle a little screaming, can't we?"

Silence filled the room. I couldn't have said it better myself. Your ability to calm yourself down, even while your children seemingly go out of control, is the best way to set the table. Only then can you make decisions out of integrity. Only when you're calm can you decide what appropriate consequence needs to be enforced in response to that behavior. That's where we're headed next.

Reflection Questions

1. What images come to mind when you think about "putting a child in his place"?

2. How much do your kids need to respect you in order for you to exercise your authority? What are ways you can act to earn that respect?

3. What family rituals would you like to implement? Which ones are you already doing that you would like to see continue?

4. What do you allow to prevent you from fully accepting your role as the one in charge?

5. Name a parent you know who does a great job at balancing authority and respect. What about that parent inspires you to find a similar balance?

Chapter Nine

Let the Consequences
Do the Screaming

If I had to live my life again,
I'd make the same mistakes, only sooner.
—Tallujah Bankhead

A life spent making mistakes is not only
more honorable but more useful
than a life spent doing nothing.
—George Bernard Shaw

As parents, we have within our reach the greatest and most effective disciplinary strategy in the history of the world. Let's make it even more grandiose. We have at our fingertips the most powerful teaching method ever devised or discovered. No, it is not military school. The single greatest teaching and discipline strategy is a phenomenon embedded within the fabric of life itself.

Simply put, here it is: our choices have consequences. Every single one of them. It is a bedrock truth in life.

You know about this on several levels. You've seen the ripple effect of the smallest drop falling into a lake, for instance, and you've heard the notion about the mere flap of a butterfly's wings leading to a hurricane across the globe. Every action we take has come in response to a million actions before it and therefore leads to another million actions afterward.

> All of our choices have consequences. This is a bedrock truth in life.

Do you know what commands the most respect in a leader? (Hint: it's the same quality that leads to the personal maturity of self-directed people.) The quality that commands the most respect is an ability to accept responsibility for your actions, regardless of the factors leading up to those actions. This is what we all want for our kids. We want our children to see their spot in the world and be aware of all the influences upon their choices. And in light of all that, we want them to take personal responsibility for their choices and accept with dignity the repercussions, the consequences of those actions. You make a choice, you accept the consequences of that choice—good or bad. That's the type of maturity we want for our children. That's the self-direction we've been talking about.

Well, here's the good news and the bad news. Good news: Like I stated earlier, the primary vehicle for nurturing that type of maturity in your child is at your very fingertips. It is bigger than you, more powerful than you and it is always ready for action. You want your child to grow up and accept the consequences for their actions? Then all you have to do is welcome those consequences into your home. It's really that simple.

Here's the bad news: If you start to welcome consequences into your home, you have to first learn to accept those consequences for yourself. And we humans have been avoiding those since back in the Garden of Eden. But you choosing to read this book means you are willing to accept the consequences of your actions. You are already growing in that ability. But now it gets even tougher—you have to learn to watch your children suffer through *their* consequences.

The Truth About Consequences

Marianne, a single mother of four, was engaged in a frustrating pattern with her fourteen-year-old daughter, Julia. Seems that mornings were getting harder and harder for both of them. They lived within walking distance of Julia's school, but Julia preferred to catch a ride with Mom on her way to work. Every morning Julia whined and stalled and Mom reacted by nagging and screaming. This pattern, not unlike the one you may have enjoyed this very morning with your child, had been going on for a long time. And it was destroying their relationship. But one morning, instead of screaming and nagging, Marianne decided to focus on herself. She decided to stop her part of the pattern.

This was her proclamation: "Julia, I'm leaving in ten minutes. If you're not ready to go, I'm still leaving. It's your choice whether you want to ride with me or not."

This wasn't a loud, boisterous threat, nor was it an anxious plea to comply for Mom's sake. Marianne simply stated her intentions in a calm, clear voice. In the process, she highlighted Julia's own choice in the matter.

You can guess what happened next. Ten minutes came and Marianne went. Julia had to fend for herself. The way Marianne tells it, she didn't even really think about Julia until she got the phone call around noon.

"Mom, what can I eat for lunch?"

"Don't you have your lunch money for the cafeteria?"

"I'm not at school, Mom. You left me at home, remember?" Her attitude was very "entitled."

"You are going to walk to school right now, Julia, and I will not write you a note. You will take an unexcused absence. You'd better go now so you don't have too many missed assignments. Bye now."

And then she hung up. And didn't call back to check up on her daughter. She returned her focus toward herself and what she needed to accomplish at work.

Once home, Marianne learned that Julia did go to school and she did take an unexcused absence. According to the school rules, that meant she would have to take a zero on every assignment she missed. Good, Marianne thought, Julia would get to learn a lesson about personal responsibility.

Julia complained and pouted, but it wasn't that much of a protest. She was too excited about going to the homecoming dance on the following night—a hugely important occasion in Julia's young life.

And that's where the story gets really interesting. You see, Julia's unexcused absence was on Thursday before the Friday night dance. Although Julia was aware of one of the consequences of having an unexcused absence (the zero on missed assignments), she was not aware of another consequence: If a student has an unexcused absence the day before or the day of a school event, that student is not allowed to participate in the school event.

No homecoming for Julia.

You can imagine Julia's response. Wailing, screaming, anguish. Of course, she blamed Mom. Mom could have waited on her that morning. Mom could have written her a fictitious note the next day. Maybe Mom still could. Even Julia's older brother sympathized with his sister's plight. He was the oldest and according to Marianne, he and Julia hadn't gotten along in years. Now here he is, carrying a sobbing little sister in his arms, pleading with Mom to intervene with the school.

Can you feel Marianne's dilemma here? She was excited she had finally held firm, refusing to give in to Julia's pleadings that morning. This had been a tired pattern and she had finally decided to focus on herself instead of trying in vain to change her daughter. She had acted with integrity. Julia had decided to call her bluff, but then refused to take responsibility. Marianne could have reacted the same way as she had previously—more nagging and screaming, then finally caving in—but she didn't. She chose to stop her part of the pattern, to stop acting as if Julia had no choice in the matter. Julia did have a choice in the matter and that choice had consequences either way. With this realization, Marianne was setting Julia's *place*. What Julia did with that choice, what she did with her *space*, was up to her.

But now Julia and her brother and sisters (and her date!) didn't see it that way. Now they all just wanted Mom to cave in and fix the situation, to do whatever it would take to help Julia escape her fate. And they were all furiously screaming for Mom to intervene.

In the face of all this fury, here were the questions Marianne faced. They are, indeed, all the questions you must face as you welcome choice and consequences into your parenting. First, did the punishment fit the crime? Well, what was the crime here? Taking too much time to get ready in the morning? Disrespecting her mother's own time requirements? Choosing to stay at home when she could have easily walked?

> The more our children are exposed to the small consequences of their small infractions, the less they will have to commit large infractions and experience large consequences.

So does Julia deserve to miss the dance? That's the emotional way of asking the question. And that's the way the kids kept asking it.

Here's the principled way: Is missing the homecoming dance a natural or logical consequence of Julia's choice? The school believed so. And that's a real issue here.

Consequences are not just the domain of parents. The consequences for our kids' choices are not just in our hands; as they get older they belong more and more in the hands of other authorities. This case was not entirely within Marianne's jurisdiction.

Here is where it is important to learn Ron Rose's "inoculation" theory about consequences. Rose, in his book *Common Sense*

Discipline, wisely asks us to remember how everyone becomes immune from polio—we each take a small dose of polio. The same is true with consequences. The more our children are exposed to the small consequences of their small infractions, the less they will have to commit large infractions and experience large consequences. The sooner we can expose our children to the universal law of sowing and reaping (at whatever age they happen to be right now), the less they will need to have the larger consequences teach them as they get older. That's the idea.

As your kids get older, the realm of authorities they report to becomes larger than just Mom and Dad. And the consequences from those authorities become more severe. That's when you as a parent have to discern whether we can and/or should intervene.

For Marianne to intervene and interrupt the process, she would have had to compromise her integrity. Here's why. She would have to go back on her statement to her daughter. She would have to lie to the school and tell them Julia was sick. Marianne decided to ask herself what the consequences would be of her own decision. With either decision (caving in or holding firm), what would she teach her daughter about life and how it works? With either decision, what would she teach her daughter about their relationship? Most importantly, with either decision, what would Marianne teach her whole family about her own level of self-respect?

Protecting vs. Exposing: The Real Struggle

We don't like to watch our children make mistakes. And we don't like having to take the time and energy to enforce the consequences. So instead, we scream. We threaten. We hope it works, meaning we hope our screaming forces them to behave the way we need them to. When it doesn't, we scream some more—and then our screaming becomes the consequence itself. This isn't working and everyone knows it. No one is learning or growing through this process, but what else can you do?

You can let the consequences do the screaming. You can learn to get out of the way and let the consequences do their job. So how do you do that? Well, you can guess the answer: learn to calm yourself down. But before you do that, you must actively become interested in calming yourself down, instead of focusing on getting your children to stop making mistakes.

So here's a question to help you confront your own anxiety. How do you balance protecting your kids from life's dangers and yet exposing them to life's lessons? This is not only a tough question, but I believe this is also the most important question for you to constantly keep before you. The answer will change depending on each child, each situation and each developmental stage, but the question never changes.

For instance, you're not going to expose a two-year-old to the consequence of getting hit by a car in order to teach him not to play in the street. But what about when he's seventeen? He'll be in the street all the time, behind the wheel in the most dangerous form of transportation on earth. And you can't be with him all the time. Sure, you could anxiously worry and pray he never gets into an accident or never gets a ticket. But remember the inoculation theory. The earlier he gets exposed to life's lessons, the less likely he will need the school of hard knocks later down the road.

But some of us give in to our anxiety so deeply and so often we always answer the question the same way: I'm going to protect my child from every danger, even if it means denying them the experience of learning from experience.

I love the part in Disney/Pixar's *Finding Nemo* when Nemo's dad laments losing his son.

He says to Dory, the fish helping him find Nemo, "But I promised him that nothing bad would ever happen to him!"

After a wonderful pause, Dory tells the truth. "Well, that was a dumb thing to do."

Our anxiety tells us to protect our children at all costs. Do whatever it takes to ensure they make it out of our responsibility alive and well. Our anxiety tells us the worst thought imaginable is for our child to experience pain, so we had better do whatever it takes to avoid that. Even if it means overprotecting them. Even if it means smothering them and never letting them out of our sight. Even if it means neglecting to enforce consequences. Even if it means helping them avoid consequences.

As a high-school teacher, my wife has the privilege of working with some incredibly bright, gifted, and overachieving teenagers. The pressure is high for these kids and for their parents as well. What never ceases to amaze her, however, are the lengths some parents will go in order to prevent their child from having to suffer clear consequences for their choices. Whether it be begging and pleading for an extended deadline or actually finishing their teenager's work, some highly reactive parents will do almost anything to prevent their child from experiencing consequences. The true irony is that in the name of their child's education, these parents are denying their children the chance to learn! Learning from their mistakes is the most effective form of education possible!

I recently heard a story about a father who obviously could not stand the thought of his son having to learn through suffering. His son had a reputation, even among his friends, as a reckless driver. After one more ticket, a speeding violation for going 75 m.p.h. in a 35 m.p.h. speed-limit zone, the son's license was surely in jeopardy. That's when Dad's anxiety took over.

Turns out Dad was a judge and he decided to use his influence to "make the ticket go away."

This kid's friends now say he's driving worse than ever. They're actually afraid to ride with him and they fear "he's going to kill somebody."

Calming Our Anxiety While Watching Their Mistakes

I think Billy Joel said it very well. Mistakes, in the end, are the only things we can truly call our own. There is a certain dignity in learning from our choices. We made the choice to stay out late and we now get the experience of getting grounded as a result. There is a sense of pride there.

But most of us would love it, absolutely love it, if our children could learn without making mistakes. Think of how appealing that is. They would always act wisely, they would never have to go through the pain and anguish of walking through tough lessons and they would absolutely love and respect our wisdom and experience. Therefore, we would never have to console them when we want to strangle them, we would never have to enforce restrictions that actually restrict us, and we would never have to watch our children make our same mistakes. And that last part is a huge part of it. How many times have we heard (or said!) the following two sentences:

1) I don't want my kids to make the same mistakes I made.

2) I just want my kids to have some respect for my wisdom and experience.

Those would both be among the top desires of all parents, particularly those trying to raise teenagers. It is so infuriating for parents to watch their kids make a stupid decision that could have so easily been avoided! We know firsthand, so many times, about the logical consequences of a particular choice, and if our child would have just sought our wisdom or listened to our advice, they wouldn't have to go through whatever's coming next. And we wouldn't have to go through it either.

Where do you want to be when your child makes a mistake?

Wouldn't it just be easier if they chose to call before they came in late? Wouldn't it be wiser to ask us for help before they tried to fix the overflowing toilet? Wouldn't it have avoided all this unnecessary pain if they would have just turned in their homework on time? We could have avoided all of this!

Calming ourselves down while we watch our children choose poorly is about as difficult as it gets. It's also our most important task if we are to retain any influence in our relationships with our kids. So what happens when they do stupid things? Make stupid mistakes? We panic. We get reactive. We scream. And remember, what we're screaming is—regardless of the words coming out of our mouths—CALM ME DOWN! I can't handle it that you've done this and I can't handle the fact that now I'm going to have to clean up your mess! Get out of the way!

But think for a moment about where you want to be when your child makes a mistake (and they consistently will). Where do you want to be in relation to them? Do you want to be standing over them, waiting for them to admit their mistake, show remorse and acknowledge you were right? That's where you are whenever you need to say four of the most damaging words in any relationship: "I told you so." I'm standing above you, waiting for you to acknowledge me as vindicated and validated! And then we complain when our kids won't talk to us about their problems or lie to us about their choices. No wonder.

But perhaps you want to choose to be somewhere else in relation to them. Perhaps you choose the other extreme position, under them. This is when you choose to help them escape the consequences, whether actively (fighting the school) or passively (neglecting to enforce your own house rules). You are beneath them, hoping they learn by the close call they avoided and hoping they never do that again. And then you complain they don't respect you or ever come to you seeking wisdom. Why should they? You're beneath them! They only come to you seeking rescue.

Choosing to welcome consequences in your home enables you to take a different position altogether. Choosing to welcome consequences is choosing to become a life guide for your children, walking alongside them as they struggle and suffer. You position yourself as a leader who operates in reality. You recognize the law of sowing and reaping is bigger than you, bigger than your child's emotional explosions, and bigger than your anxiety.

That's the position Marianne, the single mom we looked at earlier, decided to occupy. She chose to stay calm, stay committed to her decision, and stay connected to her daughter through the painful process. Even as Julia wailed with anguish and seethed with contempt, Marianne remained ScreamFree. She did not preach, she did not blame, she did not tell Julia to calm down. Instead, she spoke with calm clarity about her position, her own hurt for Julia's situation, and her availability if Julia needed a hug. She even offered to take Julia and her date to the movies.

Consequences are a constant source of truth, experience, and education. They often hurt and lead us to feel pain, embarrassment, and regret. But they are here to help us and they are available to help you raise your children.

Reflection Questions

1. How do you balance protecting your child from life's dangers and yet exposing them to life's lessons?

2. Recall an instance from your childhood when you learned a difficult lesson by walking through the consequences of your actions. What did you learn? Who was there with you, helping you to walk through it?

3. What are some mistakes you would actually like to see your child commit? Why? What might he/she learn through the experience?

4. What mistakes would you like to see your child avoid at all costs? Why? How anxious do you feel at the very thought of these mistakes?

5. For you, what is the hardest part about enforcing consequences?

Chapter Ten

Empty Threats Are Really Broken Promises

*To what extent are children "spoiled" by material gifts
and to what extent are they spoiled by their parents'
failure to make them responsible for the consequences
of their own behavior?*
—Edwin H. Friedman, *Friedman's Fables*

On my daughter's next birthday, my family is getting a dog. I know this for a fact. This is not a prophecy and it is not idle speculation. This is ironclad, 100-percent guaranteed fact.

How do I know this to be true?

On that day, my daughter will turn eight years old and in our family, "we keep our promises."

It seems a few years ago, "someone" promised a pleading little girl that "when you're old enough to help take care of it" we would add a canine to the family. I say "someone" because I like to think it was my wife who made this promise. That way I can blame her when the beast poops in the living room.

Now maybe this promise to a little girl was made after long sessions of careful planning, after hours of deliberate conversation between her parents, and after clear consideration of all possible ramifications.

Yeah, right.

More likely it came as a promise uttered in haste, in an attempt to deal emotionally with an anxious situation. "When you're old enough" is a great way to prolong the inevitable or assuage the tears of a beautiful little girl.

So, since this idle promise was offered in haste and so far in advance, I can easily back out, right? I mean, we don't have the space for a dog, or we don't have the right backyard, or I can't be held to a promise I had to make just to avoid breaking my daughter's heart. Surely there's someway I can back out and still keep my integrity. I just have to blame my responses on the whims of a little girl.

No. We will get a dog next year, simply because it was a promise. And, as both my children routinely remind me, "we keep our promises." We keep them even though they were made in haste, with little forethought and done in an effort to emotionally deal with an anxious situation.

A Word About Communication

"But you promised!"

I guarantee you've heard those words at least once from each of your kids in the past year. And they usually hurt. Those three little words carry such pain and disillusionment.

Let's focus on that word disillusionment. One of the processes involved in our kids' launch into adulthood is leaving the illusion of our perfection. When little, our kids have to hold us up as perfect because that is what they need us to be. It's a safety net. What they know is that all they need is provided (or not provided) by their parents, the All Powerful. Little kids need their parents to be big and powerful, because when you're as short as a two-year-old, someone has to protect you. Kids need to be able to trust their parents, trust they'll be able to slay the dragon in the closet or the monster under the bed. And they need to be able to believe what their parents say is true. If they can't trust their parents, their guardians against evil, what kind of a world is it?

Let's take a step back and talk for a moment about communication. I know, every therapist always wants to talk about communication, but I want to try to simplify it. All communication comes down to two parts: what gets said and what gets received. What gets said refers to the actual words spoken or written. What gets received refers to the entire message and its effect on the relationship between the parties involved.

When I make a promise to my daughter about getting a pooch, what gets said is the stuff about the dog. What gets received is the dynamic between me, my daughter, and the rest of my family. By holding myself to a promise, even a promise I may want to take back, I create a dynamic that far supersedes even the happiness (or misery) of picking up poop. By keeping that promise, here's what gets communicated:

- The world has a certain order to it;
- People are accountable to one another;
- Authority can be trusted;
- Words and actions have meaning and power; and
- In this crazy and chaotic life, promises still matter.

And to a little girl, when her daddy shows all of this to her, what she understands is she still matters. That's what gets communicated with every promise we make, hold ourselves to, and then keep. And all those critical life lessons get taught without ever having to preach any of them. Just keep your promises, and those lessons teach themselves.

Another Kind of Promise

Makes promise-keeping pretty important, doesn't it? Now comes another wrinkle in the quest to become and stay ScreamFree. As challenging as it is, that entire process happens just as effectively, just as powerfully, when those promises are promises for something other than gifts. That process and those lessons get communicated just as wonderfully when the promise is to enforce the consequences of breaking the rules.

That's right: "if you do that again you will lose your Game Boy for two days" is just as much a promise as "when you turn eight years old, we will get a family dog."

It comes down to integrity. It's very important your children believe what you say.

I cannot stress enough what unfortunate consequences—long and short term—you and your kids will have to endure if they learn you can't be taken for your word. At the same time, I cannot stress enough how revolutionary your relationships become when your kids know they can trust your word *no matter what*. It comes down to integrity—meaning what you say, saying what you mean and following through with what you promise. The sooner you begin to incorporate this principle into your bones, the sooner you will begin to see revolutionary transformations. For instance, think about the difference it would make if your kids knew for a fact, from repeated experiences, that you never give second warnings.

But not all of us are ready to be taken at our word when it comes to the business of setting and enforcing consequences. Susan liked to make big threats to her kids. She's a comedian by nature and everything she says and does tends to be funny. Her husband knows it, her kids know it, and as soon as I started coaching her, I knew it. This sometimes made our work together a true joy. But sadly, this tendency toward silly humor made it difficult for any of us to take anything Susan said seriously. How could we?

> It comes down to integrity—meaning what you say, saying what you mean, and following through with what you promise.

Once, I got to witness an effort to address her son's behavior. As this seven-year-old kept pestering his mommy, this is what came out: "If you don't stop, I'm going to saw your butt off with a plastic spoon."

This threat was received with peals of laughter from everyone within earshot (including me). I could only wonder how her kids differentiate between her jokes and her serious comments. Needless to say, this particular threat didn't have much of an influence on her young son.

What this reflected is a subtle way of trying to avoid the business side of parenting—addressing serious issues in non-serious ways. Again, we simply don't like to do the dirty work and we wish we didn't have to. We get so aggravated our verbal instructions aren't enough to modify our child's behavior that we resort to whatever means available.

For Susan, that meant using a humorous threat that carried no serious weight behind it. What she hoped was the resulting laughter might do the trick. You can imagine the uphill climb Susan faced as she began to mean what she said and say what she meant. Her kids refused to believe her at first and Susan struggled with giving up altogether. That's the way it always is when we start to change our part of a pattern. The others around us don't know what to expect, so they crank up their efforts to bring us back to the old way of doing things—even if the old way wasn't very effective. But Susan found out, as I'm confident you will, that patterns are patterns and all patterns, with persistant self-direction, can change.

Another coaching client, Thomas, eventually learned the power of keeping his promises in order to change a pattern, but he had a different pattern to overcome. His part of the pattern centered on his reluctance to keep himself to his own promises. Thomas was having huge problems with his teenage son. The problems became so serious that the son was placed on some major restrictions. All of that was appropriate and could have been effective except but for one huge detail. My client refused to set a date or condition for the restrictions to end. When pressed, he responded he didn't want his son to hold him to anything. He didn't want his son to comply for a certain amount of time just to end the restrictions. Here's the problem—the son had no idea where he stood. The son was left feeling more resentful because Dad would not hold himself to any stated condition. Talk about a power struggle! The father had the ultimate power and the son had absolutely no tools with which to fight. He was left not having a clue about his place in the universe. Not to mention he was losing trust in his father's word.

Your kids actually want you to hold firm—how else can they grow to trust you, others, God, and the universe if they cannot depend (sometimes begrudgingly) on your consistent follow-through?

The Power of Consistency

"What you reap is what you sow."

"You made your bed, now you're going to have to lie in it."

"For every action, there is an equal and opposite reaction."

We love these expressions because they seem to reflect some bedrock principle of the universe. You can find expressions of it in all of the most revered spiritual texts and most studied philosophies. But these philosophies aren't solely applicable to the one receiving the consequences. They also apply to you.

Be consistent and remember it will maintain stability in your world. Be consistent and it becomes easier to remain ScreamFree. And in turn, remaining ScreamFree makes it easier to remain consistent. Here are some principles to help guide your way:

1. Don't ever set a consequence that is tougher for you to enforce than it is for them to endure.

How serious can you possibly be by grounding your teenage daughter for two months? Are you crazy? Do you really think it's possible to babysit her that long? What about taking TV away from your five-year-old for an entire week? What? That's one of your babysitters! Do you really want to have that much more pressure to entertain him? When we overextend ourselves, it becomes that much easier to cave in when the emotional pressure hits. And thus, we break our promises and we break the finely knit fabric of trust.

2. There are no shortcuts to setting or enforcing consequences.

Providing consistent discipline for our children is always time-consuming, sometimes exhausting, and never done from afar. That's right, it's supposed to be difficult. Remember, nothing asks us to grow up like helping our children grow up. And seeking to discipline with ruthless consistency is asking yourself to grow up. It takes more time than you have available, more energy than you think possible, and more strength in the face of constant criticism than you think you can muster. But I know you can do it and in fact, you already are. Reflect on the times when you have been consistent, when you have followed through. I guarantee you've been able to do it more than you think you have. Keep it going.

3. Only choose consequences you are willing to enforce.

At first glance, this statement may sound redundant. Or ridiculous. How can I choose something I'm not willing to enforce? Easy, actually. Let your anxiety choose it for you. Here's what I mean. I am not going to tell you whether to employ timeouts or spankings or charts or any other particular consequence. So many people constantly ask me about these different techniques and my answer is always the same: what do you think? I know this point will sound like therapy-speak, but I want my purpose to be clear.

What you do is not nearly as important as how and why.

What is your motivation for spanking? Look down deep, focus on yourself and honestly answer the question. Why do you want to spank your child? If you say you do not want to, but you believe it is needed, then you are not acting with integrity.

A ScreamFree parent never does something she doesn't want to do. You are an adult and you make every choice you make. If you spank without wanting to, then you need to focus on yourself some more. Why would you choose a consequence for your child if you did not want to choose it? Because he needed it? For what? Behavior modification? To calm him down? To show him who's boss? Again, I'm not saying spanking is necessarily bad. I'm saying in order for any enforced consequence to have its desired effect, it needs to come from the solid, principled decision of its enforcer. If you're wishy-washy about spanking, that will get communicated very clearly. And here's what you'll communicate: I am at my wits' end here, son, and I do not know what else to do but resort to the most base-level power I have over you, my physical size and strength.

As you've learned throughout this book, what that really communicates is that your anxiety is really driving the boat. And if anxiety is driving the boat, then we are not really in charge. A relationship can only take so many anxiety-driven interactions before becoming an anxiety-driven relationship. This means power struggles, scream-fests and/or long periods of distance and silence.

4. Only choose consequences you are willing to endure yourself.

A coaching client, Dan, had a recent experience with a traffic ticket. Both he and his teenaged son had received speeding tickets in the same month. Dan was confused whether to tell his son about his own ticket. This was his son's third in the past year, which would likely cost him his license for a few months. Dan was understandably upset, but he wrestled with how upset he could possibly be, given his own speeding infraction.

"I taught him how to speed. I should probably teach him how accept the consequences."

Dan was so tempted to rescue his son, because a suspended license would upset the entire family system's schedule. You see, Dan Jr. and his two younger sisters all attend the same private school. And Jr. had been driving all three of them to school every morning. With a suspended license for Jr., Dan Sr. would be the one to get them all to school for the rest of the year. That's a big disruption.

Dan Sr. was thus tempted to rescue both himself and his son. He found a lawyer who, for a large fee, "could make both tickets go away." This was incredibly appealing. Dan could avoid any consequences for his own infraction and could avoid having to drive his whole family around for several months.

But like Marianne, the single mom in the previous chapter, Dan was starting to grow. His integrity would not let him make such a cowardly choice. Calming his own considerable anxiety instead, he chose to first accept the consequences of his own mistake, even taking his son with him to his own court appearance. He then walked alongside his son as he went through his court appearance.

All these practical principles are dependent upon one thing: staying calm. Consistent enforcement of consequences is the single most effective application of authority in the parent-child relationship. But only if you can calmly think through your decisions before you make them. Then you greatly increase the chances that those decisions will be sensible, realistic, and helpful in facilitating everyone's growth.

Stay consistent with your words, yes; but most importantly, stay consistent with yourself. Even if it means choosing some discomfort and inconvenience. As for me, I'll be getting a dog next year and all the responsibility that dog ownership implies. And that's okay.

Thank God I didn't promise her a cat.

Reflection Questions

1. How well did your parents keep their promises and follow through on their warnings? What did their consistency (or lack thereof) teach you about trust, authority, and the ways of the universe?

2. When are you most prone to make threats you don't keep? What effects on your parent-child relationships have you seen from your inconsistency?

3. What consequences are you the most consistent with on a regular basis?

4. How might your increased consistency improve your relationships with each of your children?

5. How does remaining ScreamFree help you stay consistent? How does staying consistent help you remain ScreamFree?

Storytime

___

This story involves a teenager, Julie, making the mistakes of, well, a teenager. Her actions are really nothing new. The response of her parents, Mark and Jennifer, however, is remarkable. Jennifer's choices display to us all the incredible power of keeping our cool, and their family revolution is well under way.

Julie was thoroughly looking forward to her birthday. Not only would turning sixteen mean finally getting her driver's license (after a year with a learner's permit), but it also meant a ten-day trip to Europe with her favorite aunt. For all of her fifteenth year, Julie had eagerly anticipated the trip. She also eagerly anticipated getting rid of her learner's permit and finally getting her own driver's license. As with most learners' permits, hers dictated she could only drive with a licensed adult in the passenger's seat. Her parents' insurance went a step further, dictating she could only drive one particular car.

As Julie's birthday approached, the Europe plans came into place. Ten days on "the Continent" promised for an amazing trip indeed.

A month before the trip, however, Julie had to make the phone call all of us parents dread: "Mom and Dad, I've been in an accident."

Arriving upon the scene, Mark and Jennifer remained calm. Their only concern was their daughter's safety. Holding her safely in their arms, they could then learn the details. Julie's boyfriend was driving his car with Julie in the passenger's seat. He lost control and struck a tree. The car was mangled, but both kids escaped with only minor cuts and bruises. The police took down the details, the insurance company started their process and everything slowly went back to normal—until three days before the trip to Europe.

Racked with guilt, and apparently growing more confident in her parents' calm resolve, Julie decided to make her confession.

"Mom, Dad, *I* was the one driving the car. We lied to you guys and to the police so I wouldn't get in trouble."

So what can a ScreamFree parent do here? What type of emotional reactions come to the surface? What would you feel? Infuriated? Disappointed? Would you feel torn, impressed on the one hand your daughter confessed at all and yet manipulated on the other hand, knowing that with three days before the Paris trip it would be difficult to cancel plans?

Mark and Jennifer felt all of these, which left them feeling more confused than anything else. With an amazing self-awareness, they knew they needed to turn to principles more than emotions. They knew they needed to ask themselves that critical question: How do we balance protecting our child from life's pains and yet exposing our child to life's lessons? After much reflection, they finally made their decision.

With the calm of a strong and loving mom and dad, they approached their daughter with nothing but well-wishes. They decided to send her off to Europe with warm embraces and hopes she would have the time of her life.

When she asked about the car and her license and all of that, Mark calmly responded, "We'll have plenty of time to deal with that when you get back. Now let's get you ready to celebrate your sixteenth birthday, Princess, by sending you to Paris."

While in Paris, Julie's guilt would creep up and she would call her parents in tears.

Resisting the urge to tell her, "Well, you should feel guilty, young lady! Here we are spending all this money and blah, blah, blah," Mark and Jennifer spoke of nothing but their fondest feelings. They would ask her about all she was seeing and doing and when she would stop and tell them how sorry she was, they would just ask her to tell them more about Europe.

But what about when she got home? How long did it take them to lay down the hammer? Julie's parents decided to wait two full days after she returned before addressing the situation. They got her pictures developed, they looked at souvenirs and they talked and talked about Paris. After two days, her parents then set a meeting and they had a long discussion about how to proceed.

Mom and Dad informed Julie she was going to inform the police and the insurance company about her lie. Mark had spoken with a lawyer and was thus fully informed about the possible ramifications. He had learned this may have meant she would have to wait until her eighteenth birthday to apply for a license. It may have meant another learner's permit after that. Mark and Jennifer knew this could all result in a major inconvenience for the whole family. But they also knew they would stand right beside Julie the entire time, helping her walk through these tough consequences with dignity.

You can only imagine what this has done for their relationship with their daughter. It has been revolutionary, to say the least.

Section Four

———

Putting Yourself into Practice

Our children are watching us live, and what we ARE shouts
louder than anything we can say.
—Wilfred A. Peterson

Doctors, psychologists, and yes, family therapists all have a word to describe their careers. These professionals do not operate a *perfect*, they operate a *practice*. This is not because they aren't professionals; it is because they have such a profound respect for the immense learning curve involved in attempting such professions. These practitioners are just that, practitioners, because the learning curve never ends—they never stop actively working on themselves and their work. They are always practicing, never getting to the point where they no longer need to work on their game.

And that's what ScreamFree Parenting is all about—learning to develop a practice. This is not about figuring it all out or devel-

187

oping the right techniques for every situation. It is certainly not about eliminating your mistakes as a parent. ScreamFree Parenting is about continuing a journey toward integrity. This is a journey of learning to live according to principles, not techniques. This is a journey of constant learning and growing, refusing to ever believe you've made it or you can't learn anything else.

I hope that you, by reading this book, have begun a journey of listening more and more to your core principles and less and less to your anxious reactivity. That is the result of learning to calm down. In this next section, you will learn how to best begin that journey. While this journey involves focusing more on yourself, the blessings that come from this journey are not just for you, but for all those around you. The types of intimate, enjoyable, cooperative relationships you crave are waiting for you along this journey. These relationships won't develop automatically and they won't come quickly. But you are on a path that makes these relationships possible, and all the more likely.

> ScreamFree Parenting is not a problem-solving or behavioral modification model, it is a growth model.

There's another helpful expression about practice. We often hear, usually in association with sports, that "practice makes perfect."

No, it doesn't.

It is far more accurate that "practice makes permanent." What you practice over and over again gets ingrained as a pattern, and bad patterns are probably one of the reasons why you're reading this book. Therefore, developing a practice is recognizing you are always, always participating in either the creation of a new pattern or the continuation of an old pattern. What's great is knowing you can change any relational pattern by simply changing your part. Practice changing your part and watch the changes begin around you.

Finally, please look carefully at the title for this section. You might expect a self-help or parenting book to say something like "Putting the Lessons (or Techniques) into Practice." That is not the emphasis of this section, or this book. At the end of the day this is all about you, putting all of yourself into your relationships, particularly those you enjoy with your children. This is about seeing your parenting as an engagement of yourself with each of your children as separate, growing people. ScreamFree Parenting is not a problem-solving or behavioral modification model, it is a growth model. It is a growth model that begins first and foremost with you. And you are already growing more than you think.

I urge you to dive into this next section with one vision in mind: taking care of yourself is your number one responsbility to your family. As I hope you will see, the best way to put yourself into the practice of parenting is to make sure you are operating with the most healthy *self* you can be. I believe this is the great news you've been waiting to hear ever since you became a parent— it's okay to want to take care of yourself first. Not only is it okay, it is the most important thing you can do in order to raise loving, responsible, and self-directed kids.

Chapter Eleven

Put on Your Own Oxygen Mask First

Self-love, my liege, is not so vile a sin
as self-neglecting.
—William Shakespeare, *Henry V*

Fritz and Tami Miller, business partners and dear friends of mine, recently returned from China with their first child, Talia YuSe. This meant spending countless hours in preparation for the trip over there, the legal dealings with the Chinese government, and the long but glorious trek home with their new little girl.

What they hadn't prepared for was the fact that eighty-seven other newly adopted Chinese babies and their new parents would also be on the fifteen-hour plane trek as well.

Now, my friends made it home all right with no permanent damage, but I can only imagine the look on the poor, frazzled flight attendant's face as she began to deliver her safety routine with eighty-seven adopted babies and their scared new parents staring back at her.

As the instructions began in monotone Chinese followed by monotone English, most people tuned her out.

> You cannot take care of your family unless you first tend to yourself.

"Be sure your seat belt is properly fastened . . . Locate the exit nearest you . . . In case of an emergency, use your seat cushion as a flotation device . . . In the event of a sudden loss of cabin pressure, oxygen masks will deploy. Place the mask over your mouth and nose and breathe normally. If you are traveling with an infant or a small child, *be sure to secure your own oxygen mask first.*"

Suddenly, many of these new parents perked up. The familiar phrase suddenly takes on a whole different meaning with a new little life literally lying in your hands. The thought of this tiny being, completely dependent upon you, struggling for breath, is unbearable at best.

And because of the anxiety of that thought, it is far too easy to miss out on the wisdom of the flight attendant's instruction.

Without proper levels of oxygen, our brains do not function as they should. Our judgment becomes impaired and we are unable to perform the simplest of tasks. And yet what is our likely initial response if an airplane crisis occurs? You guessed it. Most of us would panic and struggle like mad to mask our children before we even give a second thought to ourselves. But here's the truth about airplane crises and about life in general, and this is the amazing wisdom from the airlines: if you're gasping for breath, you can't help anybody else.

You don't have to be in a crisis, however, to appropriate the wisdom of this statement for all of life. You cannot take care of your family unless you first tend to yourself. It's that simple. And it's vital to the health of everyone involved.

What Does It Mean to Be Selfish?

So why is our natural response to shun this thinking? I believe it is because we vastly misunderstand what *caring for yourself first* really means. Most people interpret self-love as selfishness, an obviously negative trait.

For those in religious traditions, this seems to be an especially vexing dilemma. We get caught in this trap by thinking we are facing an either/or dichotomy. Either I focus solely on myself or I focus on serving others, particularly my kids, who need me so much. Either I ramrod my way through life, looking out for Number One, or I decrease so others might increase, even if I get trampled in the process.

It seems that taking care of others necessarily means neglecting ourselves.

In discussing this with a small group of parents recently, one mother put it this way: "If I take care of me, I feel like a selfish jerk, like I'm doing something very wrong. If I focus on my kids,

I sometimes feel like a doormat, busting myself to please and serve yet feeling very unappreciated for all the sacrifices I make."

Exactly. That's the false dichotomy. That's the dilemma we all face.

"Sure, there's a part of me that would love to focus on me and my needs for a change. But I can't do that. I won't do that. It's just not Christian. Or moral. Or right. Right?"

Wrong.

Other cultures have a very different take on self-care. The Hebrew Bible and later, the Christian New Testament, seemed to take self-love for granted. One of the great commandments in the Scriptures is to "Love thy neighbor as thyself." Our culture would be in serious trouble if we put this into practice with our Western way of "loving" ourselves.

> What would it really look like to love your kids as little as you love yourself?

Think about it. What would it really look like to love your kids as *little* as you love yourself? Instead of packing a healthy lunch complete with the four food groups and a note tucked inside, you'd shove a half-eaten donut and a thermos of stale coffee in their bookbags. What would it look like if you talked to your kids like you talk to yourself after you make a mistake? Most of us would berate them over and over, calling them names and finding it incredulous that they made the same mistake yet again.

So, what's the solution? Is there another way to think about it, another way to live in our relationships? Thankfully, others before us have wrestled with this question. One fellow struggler whose thoughts are particularly helpful lived about a thousand years ago. A French monk, Bernard of Clairveaux, seriously wrestled with how to balance our relationship with ourselves and our relationship with others. He wrote his thoughts down in a work called "The Four Degrees (or Levels) of Love." His particular question was how to balance a love for self and a love for God, but I think it's extremely helpful in learning how to balance all of our relationships. Allow me to summarize his theory*:

The first level of love: "I love *me* for *my* benefit."
According to Bernard, this is the most selfish and the most infantile of the four levels. The practitioner of this level thinks, "I care for my interests alone and I am only interested in results that immediately and ultimately benefit me."

From a developmental perspective, this represents a necessary stage in our growth as individuals, whereby we learn the basic skills of survival. We cry as infants for food, for clean diapers, for comforting arms. This is natural and necessary. Unfortunately, most of us know a few adults who still function at this stage of development. And, honestly, most of us can recall many times when we ourselves have regressed to this stage. Usually this happens when we have so neglected ourselves that one day we snap and commit a remarkably selfish act that surprises even us. Clearly this is not the solution for a way out of the dichotomy.

The second level of love: "I love *you* for *my* benefit."
Bernard believed this is where most of us dwell, particularly in our relationships. Someone stuck at this level operates like

* I am extremely grateful to Dr. Carroll Osburn of Abilene Christian University for this interpretation of Bernard's work.

this: "I love you and care for you because I receive validation knowing I add value to your life. I love you because I need to in order to feel right, safe, strong, worthy."

In the words of Cheap Trick, "I need you to need me." I love you because of what our relationship does for me, making me feel valuable and necessary. It also gives me reason to expect you to recripriocate my efforts. Bernard rightly questioned whether this way of loving others can truly be considered love at all, given it is based on a hidden "quid pro quo" agenda. It's the golden rule twisted inside out. Instead of "do unto others *as you would have them* do unto you," it turns into "do unto others *so that they might* do unto you."

This is, frankly, where most of us find ourselves in all of our relationships, particularly as parents with our kids. Think back on the mother's comment about feeling unappreciated for all of her sacrifices. Who hasn't felt that way? Who hasn't wanted to quit making all these sacrifices because they keep going unrecognized and unreturned? But is that *why* we make all those sacrifices? Of course not, right? We make all those sacrifices because we love our kids!

If that's true, then what's behind our need for someone to notice? This is not about wanting appreciation, this is about needing *validation* for all of our efforts in order to feel like it's worth it to keep going at all. If others don't appreciate all my sacrifices, then why am I still making such efforts? It is because I'm stuck at the second level of love: I love *you* for *my* benefit.

The third level of love: "I love *you* for *your* benefit."

This brings us to Level Three. Bernard stated this level is deceptive because it appears to be the highest level of love and the most beneficial to the world. "I am selfless in that I am here *for* you; I am here to serve you." "None of self and all of thee," to quote an old Protestant Christian hymn. I am here to serve you and my concerns and motives do not come into the picture at all."

For a variety of reasons, this seems to be the stated and understood ideal for our relationships. We hear it in popular phrases such as, "I'll always be there for you" and "I'll do anything for you." We feel like good parents when we say to our kids, "You're the most important thing in the world to me."

Yikes! I don't want that type of pressure, do you? And if I'm just a kid, I don't want to be the most important thing in anybody's world! That's a lot of pressure to carry around, the weight of being someone's supreme significance. The truth of the matter is this level of love, while sounding elegantly selfless, can never truly exist, and thankfully so. This is the type of thinking that lauds altruism and purely unselfish motives without recognizing their impossibility. No one can ever fully take themselves and their motives out of the equation, and no one would truly want to. We want someone to serve us and treat us well because they want to, not just because we need them to.

And thinking that I can serve someone else without any motives of my own only increases the chances for my own self-deception and hidden expectations. You can see that ultimately this level of love always reverts to Level Two, for I can never fully eliminate myself and my interests and my desires. Thankfully, we just weren't made that way. Again, we want a relationship that involves someone finding their own joy in being with us, pursuing their own happiness and ours. I do not want a selfless martyr living only for me—especially not for a parent.

This brings us to Bernard's fourth and highest level of love, which he believed is the only way out of the either-me-or-you dilemma. Read this carefully, for this model of relating yourself to the world will probably sound unfamiliar and may even come across as heretical to your former way of thinking. But I believe this is the only way of relationship that makes any sense at all. Not only does it form the foundation of the entire ScreamFree philosophy, I believe it carries within it the power to create revolutionary relationships with your kids and everyone else in your world. Here goes:

The fourth level of love: "I love *me* for *your* benefit."
Read this again very carefully.

A person operating at this level says "I love me, work on me and build myself up so I can come to you from a position of wholeness, a position of fullness. *I take care of me so you don't have to.* From fullness I can then empty myself, my gifts, my love, my actions, for your ultimate benefit. I am the only one in charge of me and I am the one ultimately responsible for me and my well-being. Therefore, as a steward of my greatest gift, my life, I need to take steps to ensure my health, my calmness of mind, my sanity, and my own validation as a person in the world. Thus, I can free you from having to provide those things for me. Thus I can truly serve you without needing you to serve me."

Think of how this might radically change your relationships with your kids. You seek out your own validation from within yourself and from your Creator so that regardless of how your children feel, behave, talk, or think, you are okay and still committed to them. Think of the power in saying with all your actions, "I take care of me so that you don't have to. I don't need you to appreciate me or validate me in order for me to still take care of you."

Loving yourself first is the only true way to be ScreamFree, because it is the only way to seek first your own calm. It is the only way to truly benefit your kids without burdening them with the need to benefit you. It is not their job, nor anyone else's, to meet your emotional and physical needs. As an adult, one who is responsible to so many others you love, it is up to you to pursue your own emotional fulfillment. This doesn't mean you don't ever need other people, not by a long shot. But it does mean that your life and your health is up to you. The sooner you embrace that truth and embrace the calling to love yourself first, the sooner you can truly serve all those around you, especially your kids.

Our Cultural Confusion

I am aware that this vision of loving self to benefit others offers a radically effective alternative for how to do relationships, especially for those of us in the West. This is because we in the West suffer a profound confusion about how to relate to ourselves. Perhaps the most profound example of this confusion occurs in our bellies.

So many Westerners suffer from the rampant obesity problem. As of 2004, obesity has now surpassed smoking as America's number one health crisis, especially in its effect on the ecomony. And while there is so much attention, funding, and research on the genetic components of being overweight, the diet and exercise industry is booming as well. This is because while people are overeating, they are starving for a way to take better care of themselves.

I believe that the number one reason people are getting fatter and fatter, despite all the advancements in science and the proliferation of self-help materials, is they are struggling with the very same false dichotomy we discussed earlier.

For people to do all that is necessary in order to take better control of their weight and bodily health means learning to take better care of themselves. And in order to do that, people have to make intentional decisions to spend time, energy, and money to focus on themselves. Think about it. The only way to change your habits is to intentionally focus on yourself. But this runs counter to everything we've routinely believed about where our focus should be located. It's hard to take my focus off others, particularly my kids, when it feels like I'm being a terrible parent in order to do so. Thus we end up apologizing for having to take time out to exercise! Or feeling guilty for wanting to get away, or not cooking a big dinner, or buying healthier food at the store.

We said earlier that other cultures do not seem to share our false dichotomy. The way the Hebrews and Jesus spoke, they already assumed a strong self-love. The apostle Paul made the same assumption, at one point saying, "After all, no one ever hated his own body . . ." This was a logical conclusion at that time and in that Eastern culture.

But who do you know that *doesn't* hate their own body these days? Very few, I'm sure! Body image issues surround us so much that we cannot escape breathing in a culture of endless comparison and resulting self-hatred. The Dalai Lama spoke recently of a conference he attended back in the early 1990s. This was a conference of Western psychiatrists and psychologists discussing the issues of self-hatred. The

> Loving yourself first is the only true way to be ScreamFree, because it is the only way to seek first your own calm. It is the only way to truly benefit your kids without burdening them with the need to benefit you.

Dalai Lama said that for the first hours of listening to these doctors, he thought his broken English was failing him. He asked himself and others, "Are they really saying 'self-*hatred*?'" He says he had never, in his vast experience in Eastern philosophy and politics, even considered the notion of self-hatred. But here these doctors were speaking as if it were a very common, even epidemic condition in the West. The Dalai Lama had no folder in his mind to categorize this human experience.

But we do. We know it all too well. And in one of the most futile moves possible, we hate how we feel about ourselves, and yet we try to use that hatred to motivate ourselves to change! Let's return to the weight issue. Fat Bastard, the hugely obese Scotsman in the *Austin Powers* movies, summed it up this way: "I eat because I'm unhappy, and I'm unhappy because I eat. It's a vicious cycle."

As long as your motivation is your own self-loathing, there is no way possible to make a lasting positive change in your life. And the reason is simple. It's because the bad pattern you're trying to change, like overeating, is itself an attempt to make yourself feel better! So by trying to cut it out you are trying to cut out the only thing that makes you feel good. No wonder we sabotage our diets and exercise plans! As long as we're motivated by our self-hatred, then we'll never sustain any effort that feels like deprivation, hating ourselves more. Even if it's ultimately good for us.

This is because we don't feel we have a legitimate right to treat ourselves well in the first place. Loving ourselves, and all the effort that takes, feels far too selfish or narcissistic.

But here's what is really selfish: sacrificing yourself for the sake of others while secretly needing them to validate and reciprocate your efforts in order to keep going. And narcissism is not focusing on yourself. Narcissism is needing *others* to focus on you.

In contrast, true self-love, the "I love me for your benefit" type of love, is always seeking to truly benefit others. The person who loves herself does not need others to recognize or even love her back in order to continue. Again, she takes care of herself so that others, particularly her kids, don't have to.

That is truly loving, both to yourself and to others. That is truly being selfless.

Putting on Your Own Oxygen Mask

So, what does loving yourself look like? Well, that depends on if you choose healthy ways or unhealthy ways to do it. How do you differentiate between healthy and unhealthy ways to treat yourself? Ask yourself one simple question: "Is this activity going to *benefit* those I love?"

In order to flesh this out, let's look at the difference between an escape and a retreat. Escape is a purely selfish act in the context of relationships. Escape is an unplanned action. It is often unintentional and it is always done in haste. When you are attempting to escape from a situation, all you know is what you are running *from*—you honestly don't care to know what you're running to or why you're doing so. It is based on the need we have of self-preservation and it hardly ever involves a plan of return. At its heart, an escape is simply another form of screaming. It is an anxiety-driven reaction, and it carries all the seeds for creating the very types of relationships we're hoping to avoid.

> While people are overeating, they are starving for a way to take better care of themselves.

A retreat, on the other hand, is quite a different animal altogether. Retreats are intentional breaks from the action with the specific intent of regrouping and returning. In taking a retreat, you know where you are going and you know why you're going. You are retreating in order to benefit others as well as yourself. Retreats are a way to focus on yourself in order to become the best you imaginable. If you think this sounds selfish, consider this. Every great religious leader history can account for spent a significant amount of time in retreat before and/or during his or her service to the world. Consider Gandhi, Jesus, Paul, Muhammad, the Buddha, Mother Theresa. I'd venture a guess that not one of these figures was ever called selfish.

Here's how escape and retreat are related. *The less we take intentional retreats for ourselves, the more we will find ourselves unintentionally finding ways to escape.* If we're not diligent in carving out retreats for ourselves in the form of healthy activities, we are sure to find an escape somewhere. Escapes for you may include obvious bad habits, such as smoking, overeating or drinking to excess. You may find yourself getting completely lost in romance or fantasy novels. Or, you may mentally or even physically "check out" of your family's life.

One way to lessen the likelihood of this desire to escape is to plan intentional retreats for yourself. Pamper yourself with a manicure, learn to play a musical instrument, exercise, meditate, seek spiritual growth. Pursue profoundly deep relationships with friends outside of your family. Take your relationship with God to new heights, leaning on your Creator to provide you all the validation you need as a human being.

You may be asking yourself, "Who has the time?" You don't. That's just more evidence of the problem. You must create the time by choosing to put on your own oxygen mask first.

It is in the fabric of our culture, and it has been handed down to us from the generations, that it is far better to deny ourselves, even hate ourselves, than it is to openly love ourselves first. A full discussion of our cutural difficulty with self-hatred and self-indulgence deserves its own book, and then some. For our purposes here, I want you to think of it in very practical terms for how to accept all your responsibilty to your kids.

In an amazingly confessional interview near the end of his life, Mickey Mantle made a touching realization. In reflecting upon his broken body, disintegrated relationships (especially as a father), and premature demise, the mighty Mick sighed, "If I knew I was going to live this long, I would have taken better care of myself."

How we live today determines so much of how we will live tomorrow. And how we live today and tomorrow determines so much about our relationships with our children.

I want you to think of it this way: What has *to last* is what has *to come first.*

Your health. A broken body makes it extremely difficult to provide for and protect your children. Your health is not an "extra" in your life, it is your first responsibility.

Your self-respect. Compromising yourself by making empty threats, giving in to the whining, and rescuing your kids from consequences is not a way to build long-term relationships. It is simply a way of devaluing yourself in the eyes of your kids, and in your own. Learning to calm down and operate out of your principles is your calling as a parent, so safeguard and develop your self-respect with everything you have. Your grown children will thank you.

Your marriage. This is a huge topic for a book of its own, but know this: sacrificing your marriage for the sake of your kids will always, always end up sacrificing both.

This by no means ends the subject of taking care of yourself for the sake of your kids. What I hope this chapter can do for you is inspire you to make yourself a priority. You are so important to the world, beginning with your kids, it is imperative that you take this teaching to heart.

So go take care of yourself; we deserve you at your best.

Reflection Questions

1. What is your initial, gut-level response to the idea of taking care of yourself for the benefit of others?

2. What are some ways you have neglected your own health (physical, emotional, mental, spiritual) for the sake of your kids?

3. What is the hardest part about taking care of yourself? What do you struggle with the most?

4. Describe the self-care habits you would need to develop in order to be at your best for others.

5. What commitment to your own care are you willing to make today?

Chapter Twelve

Revolutionary Relationships

Don't you know?
Talkin' about a revolution sounds . . .
like a whisper?
—Tracy Chapman, "Talkin' About a Revolution"

Of all the chapter title decisions in this book, "Revolutionary Relationships" was the most difficult. The word "revolutionary" is thrown around so often that it often loses any meaning at all. It carries a number of applications and has found itself attached to a number of different expressions. From Marxist freedom fighters in third-world countries to the latest advancement in dishwasher detergent, "revolutionary" can describe almost anything.

What all these applications of "revolutionary" have in common, though, is the idea of a profound, effective, and lasting change. A difference that changes our lives. Revolutions are turn-arounds, upheavals, new starts. A revolution marks the beginning of the new, the creation of a reality we've only dreamed about. And I believe that's why you're reading this book. You want to turn around your relationships with your kids, creating a new revolution in your home. And that's why I'm writing this. My passion is to share the principles I believe all parents need to start revolutions in their families. These are revolutions that forever change your days and weeks, your patterns and interactions, and the futures of your children and your children's children.

> We're talking about creating *r*evolutionary relationships, making conscious choices to take hold of our own emotional reactions.

I used to employ the term "evolutionary" (without the r) to describe the possibilities of ScreamFree Parenting. I liked that the term spoke of change, of process, of something new and different emerging as a possibility. What I learned, however, was "evolutionary" carries with it a connotation connected to natural processes outside of our own conscious influence. Think evolution and you might think of the "Big Bang" theory of the origin of the universe, an event that simply happened outside of any personal intent. Well, that's not exactly what we're talking about here, is it?

We're talking about creating *r*evolutionary relationships, about making conscious choices to take hold of our own emotional reactions, taking responsibility for our own growth as parents. These are not processes outside of our influence and we are not going to simply wait for our relationships to improve! Most of us have tried that and we've learned it puts us in the unenviable position of needing everyone else to change. It doesn't work. In fact, such waiting on others has the remarkable tendency of helping to create the type of relationships we all detest.

Parenting does carry with it all the possibilities of creating evolutionary changes within us and our relationships. That is, there is a process larger than us working to transform ourselves and our relationships. But this process only works if we have the courage to consciously take hold of ourselves (and let go of others!). This happens not by accident or natural happenstance, but by conscious choices you and I make to curb our reactivity, calm our anxiety ,and respond according to our principles.

It is important to remember, though, history never saw a revolution without some form of resistance to it. And your revolution will be no different. Why is that? Why is it even terribly oppressive governments have staunch supporters and citizens willing to die for something that is clearly not intended to serve their best interests? One simple word: familiarity. When we engage in relationships, at any level, we function in a pattern with that other person, a dance, if you will. You've heard the phrase. "It takes two to tango." The same is true for relationships.

Each year, my wife begins the school year teaching a play by Henrik Ibsen, a noted Norwegian author. His play, entitled *A Doll's House*, examines the marital relationship between the two main characters, Nora and Torvald Helmer. Nora is an irritating, childlike, manipulative woman who behaves in extremely immature ways. Torvald is an overbearing and harsh husband who treats his wife like an object. Nora sneaks cookies and hides money from

Torvald. Torvald only speaks to Nora with pet names and often demeans her with insults. When my wife's students discuss these characters, they are often quick to assess blame on one character or the other for the faulty relationship. The comments usually go something like this:

"Nora is so annoying! I can't stand the way she's always dancing around the house acting like she's fourteen. No wonder Torvald treats her like a kid . . . she IS one!"

"No way! The only reason she acts that way is because of the way he treats her. He never talks to her about anything important and he's always calling her 'my little squirrel'—and 'my pet'—Puke. I don't blame her for acting selfish, he certainly doesn't seem to care about her."

Well, they're both right. Nora and Torvald are in a dance. He treats her like a child so she acts like one. She acts like a child, so he treats her as one. Trying to figure out who started the pattern is about as fruitful as discussing which came first, the chicken or the egg, or discussing which horse is the first one on a carousel. No one "started it." And it just doesn't matter. What does matter is the pattern is strong. Is it strong because both participants like the way in which it serves them? No. Its strength lies in its familiarity.

We are more comfortable in the known—even in misery—than we are in the unknown. Patterns are so powerful because they provide stability, even if that stability is wretched. So it's no wonder when one person attempts to step out of the dance and change the pattern, they will encounter strong resistance.

When you start your ScreamFree revolution in your home, your children (and maybe even your spouse) will pull out all the stops to lure you back into the dance. This is not a conscious or intentional effort on their part. And even though it may feel malicious or manipulative, trust me, it is not. It is merely a mechanism for their own survival in the family. They want things to go back to "normal," even if they hated "normal" in the first place.

But you are learning to grow yourself up, and as you grow you are able to tolerate such efforts to pull you down. A client recently told me that after an extended period of practicing ScreamFree Parenting, her thirteen-year-old finally had enough.

"I hate it when you're calm!" she screamed.

Know this: if you're getting that type of response, you are building the immeasurable type of mutual respect in your home that creates and maintains revolutionary relationships. All you have to do is stay the course—focus on

> We are more comfortable in the known—even in misery—than we are in the unknown.

yourself, grow yourself up, and calm yourself down. You will be amazed at your ability to not only implement the changes you want to make, but also to withstand any resistance to your efforts.

The Trying Threes

We are now coming to the end of the book. In an effort to keep you inspired as you begin your revolutionary journey, I want to tell you one more success story. This story takes us into that stressful phase reserved for parents and their toddlers, but with a few simple adjustments it could just as easily be a story about adolescents or teens, who are both every bit as stressful and demanding. My client Steve recently told me of an encounter with his three-year-old that remarkably illustrates the possibilities of ScreamFree Parenting. As you read about it, look for the test provided for Steve's growth in this fairly typical situation (bedtime with a three-year-old). Then look even closer for the revolution Steve's creating from the inside out by consciously deciding to stay both calm and connected.

Having recently moved across the country in order for his wife to return to work, Steve's family had seen an enormous amount of transition as of late. Everyone in the family seemed stressed, as each had to adjust to new schedules, roles, and tasks. One Sunday evening, Steve's wife had to go to the office. It was thus his job to put their three-year-old daughter, Sarah, to bed. With all the changes in the previous weeks, this had not been an easy task.

When faced with the chore of cleaning up her toys in the living room, Sarah moved into her most skillful stall tactics: acting too tired; talking in a cute, baby voice; etc. With incredible resolve, Steve refused to become reactive. He also refused to leave the scene.

As Sarah began to talk rudely to Steve, he calmly asked her, "What do you think will happen if you do that again?"

They both agreed the result would be the consequence of a time-out. He gave her the clear option of cleaning up or having a time-out and she chose to continue stalling. Steve calmly brought in her time-out chair and placed it in her room. Again, he gave her the clear choice. Sarah stalled and Steve resolutely put her in her chair. Sarah cried out, kicking and screaming. Steve offered to sit next to her, but she refused. She became vigilant against cleaning up, so Steve proceeded to tell her of the next consequences.

The bright three-year-old knew this involved putting one or more of her movies into time-out for a day, so she ran down to stand in front of the entertainment center, wanting to protect them. She assumed the stance of a hockey goalie, aiming to block any of Steve's attempts to get past her. Steve somehow managed to contain both his anger and his laughter at the situation. He calmly explained to Sarah she really could protect her videos by choosing to clean up. He then deftly managed to slip past the goalie and pulled one of the movies.

Becoming hysterical, Sarah grasped at the movie. Steve offered to let her have it if they went back upstairs, but she refused. She then went to the couch, screaming, obviously tired, still refusing to clean up. Another of her favorite movies proceeded to find itself in time-out for the next twenty-four hours. Sarah objected with more tears and Steve chose another movie.

He again stated her choice very clearly and then she did something different.

Sarah went back to the couch as before, but now she said she wanted Mommy. Here Steve faced his most difficult choice of all. He could have chosen to take such a statement personally, receiving it as an indictment of him as a parent. He could have reacted another way, choosing to force Sarah into compliance. Instead, he chose the moment as a window of opportunity to grow closer to his child. This would be a real test, one that challenged him with difficulty, but promised him great rewards for his efforts.

Steve sat beside Sarah on the couch, embraced her and created some emotional space for them both. Sarah cried out that Mommy wasn't supposed to go to work at night, that it was too dark. She wanted Mommy back home.

Steve chose to hear the plea of his daughter: "It's one thing for Mommy to go to work during the day, but she's supposed to be home when it's dark."

The recent transitions were taking their toll on a three-year-old's heart. Steve went with the momentum.

"Yeah, I miss Mommy, too. She needed some special time for herself tonight and that's okay. But I miss her, too."

The two continued an embrace for a moment or two, with Sarah beginning to calm herself and quiet her tears. Steve then offered to share a bedtime snack with her and talk about Mommy. He asked Sarah what she missed most about Mommy. Sarah stated she likes it when Mommy is home so she could "lay with me," an expression for lying down with her in her bed. Steve agreed those are special times and reiterated that while it was okay for Mommy to be gone, he missed her, too. (He couldn't help but think about how many nights his wife had had to say those same words on his behalf.) They enjoyed a bedtime snack together, with Steve setting his watch alarm to go off after a few minutes.

When it beeped, Sarah was the one who stated it was time to go clean up. Perhaps Steve's hard work was paying off. She went first and proceeded to put up her books and toys. Steve got her toothbrush ready and praised Sarah for her efforts to clean up. He even helped a little. Sarah then tried to go potty and again, Steve praised her for the effort.

Once in bed, Sarah asked Steve for a story and he spun one of his classics. Sarah's eyes began to droop and Steve began to leave, only to be hailed back with a special invitation: "Daddy, would you lay with me?"

Steve gladly accepted the request. As if that were not rewarding enough, however, Steve then experienced one of those rare moments that occasionally rewards the hard work of ScreamFree Parenting.

As he lay down, Sarah looked into his eyes and explained, "I still miss Mommy."

Choosing to remain nonreactive and to go with the momentum, Steve replied, "I know, sweetheart, I miss her, too."

Sarah then ended their dialogue with the invitation we all long for: "Daddy, would you come closer?"

He drew closer and began to stroke her blond hair. Sleep came but a few moments later.

As Steve left the room, he knew his hard work had paid off. He had not simply held his ground in the battle of attrition, as most of us try to do with our parenting, Steve had actually gained ground. He had actually used a stress-filled time as an opportunity for growth and had walked away with the invitation any parent would love to receive: "Daddy, would you come closer?"

The Revolution We All Wish For

Those are revolutionary words, especially because they came not from a manipulated and needy little girl, but from the genuine wishes of a begrudgingly respectful human being. And isn't that what we all crave in our relationships? Someone to authentically invite us closer? Isn't that the longing behind every human relationship? That someone would choose to be with us, on their own, not because we had to coerce or trick or beg them?

Think back to your own childhood years. Even then we knew what we really wanted: someone who wanted us. Remember asking our Mommy or Daddy why they loved us? Was it simply because they had to? We wanted to know we were inherently lovable, outside of some blood obligation. We wanted to know Mommy *chose* to love us; that Daddy *wanted* to be close to us. That desire hasn't gone away.

That's what we all still want most in the world, from all of our relationships: freely chosen love. And that's what we want most from and for our kids. We crave a relationship with each of our kids that springs from respect and their authentic choice, not from our heavy-handed or passive-aggressive manipulation. We also crave relationships for our kids that are models of respect and mutually chosen love. And that's revolutionary.

I firmly believe because we are talking about a *r*evolutionary relationship with each of our kids, it is possible for each and every one of us. And that means you. Regardless of your children's ages and regardless of your past mistakes, such revolutionary relationships are within your grasp!

Of course, the irony is that to grasp that type of revolution, you have to let go. It takes courage, but you must let go of your child's reactions, you must let go of your child's emotions and you must let go of your child's choices. What you must grasp in order to start a revolution is *your own* reactions, *your own* emotions, *your own* choices. "If you love them, set them free" is only half of the equation. Learning to take hold of all the responsibility it takes to be you is the real key.

You are not responsible *for* your kids, their behavior, their feelings, or any of their choices. You are responsible *to* them for *your* behavior, *your* feelings, and all of *your* choices. And every time you grasp that reality, you are indeed creating a revolution in your life, and in the world.

As I said in the very beginning, my mission is to calm the world, one relationship at a time, beginning with yours. As you take hold of the courage and confidence to become ScreamFree, please know that you are helping to calm the world. By calming yourself, you begin calming your family. And by calming your family, you begin to calm generations of the world.

May God truly bless you as you begin . . . tonight.

Reflection Questions

1. What do you think of when you hear the word "revolutionary"?

2. What type of resistance do you think you might encounter as you begin to change yourself?

3. What is one ScreamFree principle you can focus on this week? What might it look like for you to begin practicing that principle tonight?

4. What type of relationship environment do you want to create in your home? Describe each relationship and what patterns you would like to change in order to revolutionize that relationship.

Acknowledgments

At times during the writing of this book I doubted whether I would ever get to write this part. Amazingly, here I am. And of course, like every other author before and after me, I must acknowledge that writing is a team effort.

Such is ScreamFree Parenting. I started this dream way back during my family therapy internship many years ago and, thanks to so very many along the way, this book, and the company launching it, are now a solid and growing reality.

The one constant team member along the entire way is the one to whom this book is dedicated—my wife of eleven years, Jenny. She is the best friend, spouse, or parent I know, or know of. But that does not begin to acknowledge her giftedness, loyalty, support, patience, and love for me and this project. I consider her nothing less than co-creator of this material, for she has learned the principles along with me, she practices the principles better than I do, and she holds me to the principles whenever I let my anxiety get the best of me. She is an amazing co-parent, co-creator, and collaborator and I cannot thank her enough for her editing, writing, encouragement, vision, and undaunted courage.

The other team members along the way are numerous, but two in particular deserve special mention. Dave Markert, along with his wife, Dorothy, has shown a pure passion for the ScreamFree vision since he first heard me present it at a conference. Not only has he worked diligently to instill the principles into his own life and family, but also he has jumped in headfirst to help launch this company into the world. Dave, you are a brilliant businessman, an inspiring leader, and a wonderful partner. Fritz Miller, along with his wife, Tami, has been with me from the very beginning. Besides his obvious graphic design talents, Fritz demonstrates an amazingly honest and encouraging spirit. I consider you one of my closest friends, brother, and your belief in me helps keep me going.

I want to thank my newest partner as well. Jon Kaplan, along with his wife Tasha, has brought a remarkable business mind, giving us new visions of how far we can take the ScreamFree message. He has also brought a strong passion for family and friendship. Jon, welcome aboard, both as a partner and a friend.

Fernando Nasmyth has also been with me the whole way. He has shown the utmost respect for my dreams and has never shrugged off my vision for us to work together. Thank you, Fernando, for all of your support of me and my family since welcoming us to Atlanta five years ago.

The same goes for David Blackwell, Dane Booth, and John Turner. Thank you for your friendship, boys, and may Monday nights continue to celebrate more than just football.

I also want to give thanks to Roger Herring, my accountant, and Don Sloane, my personal and professional coach. Roger, you are an excellent entreprenuer, gifted thinker, and a huge support to me since the beginning. Don, you have helped me more than you know (but you hear that from all your clients!). Your encouragement, wisdom, and yes, love, have inspired me to this point. I'll see you backstage!

And two of my mentors deserve special mention: Drs. Joe Whitwell and Kerry Duncan. You both have nurtured my growth as a therapist, and I thank you for believing in me. I thank you all the more, however, for nurturing me as a man.

There are several who have actually helped with the writing of this book. Struggling to turn thoughts into pages, I leaned heavily on these gifted writers and editors to produce the best work possible. Of course, any errors belong to me, not them. John Turner, a gifted writer, thinker, and family man, helped launch the book by completing the first chapter and working on several others as well. There are phrases throughout the book that come from his ingenuity, and I am grateful. I am also grateful for his initial enthusiasm and continued encouragement, reminding me how truly revolutionary this material is. Kim Diehl, another gifted writer and editor, also helped me craft a number of the chapters, lending both her writing skills and her parenting experience to the manuscript. Kim, you were wonderful during a needy time. Thank you. Angie Fann also helped tremendously in editing and finishing the project. Angie, you were here when I needed you and you showed me more talent than I think I knew you had. My mother, Brenda Carroll, was also very gifted and generous in her proofreading and editing. Thanks so much, Mom! Finally, I must again thank Jenny, who deserves credit for at least five chapters finding their completion, with each ending up better than I thought possible. Jenny, your history professor was right all those years ago: you need to keep writing.

I could not have arrived at this point as a thinker, therapist or author without the sound theoretical and clinical base of Bowen Family Systems Theory. Dr. Murray Bowen is the most underrated thinker of the last century and his thought and practice are finally beginning to receive their due. It is my professional mission to translate Bowen's systems thinking into the working dialogue of families and organizations around the world. I am thankful to all those who have introduced and instructed me in this way of thinking, living and working with relationships. These include Drs. Waymon Hinson, Jackie Halstead and Tom Milholland of Abilene Christian University, which is, in my estimation, the finest marriage and family therapy training facility in the country. I am especially thankful to Dr. Major Boglin, now in Atlanta, who has directly instructed me in Bowen's thought and practice more than any other. Thankfully, our dialogue continues and thus, I am still growing. And, of course, I am ever grateful to those who have come after Dr. Bowen, faithfully interpreting his work as they develop their own. The world is grateful to Drs. Edwin Friedman, David Schnarch, Roberta Gilbert, Harriet Lerner, and Michael Kerr, to name a few. ScreamFree Parenting may not look like it upon first glance, but it is my first attempt to build upon your work.

To all of my therapy, coaching, and consulting clients, I give my heartfelt thanks for allowing me into your lives. Opening yourselves up to anyone is the most courageous act on earth and I am honored to have been the recipient of that privilege. Your lives have inspired me as a person and your stories throughout this book (although changed dramatically to protect your confidentiality) will inspire countless others. To all of those who have attended my seminars, thank you for your energy, your feedback, and your continued success as you revolutionize your relationships.

Finally, there have been so many believers, ambassadors, and investors so far that I feel tremendously overwhelmed. These include Don and Brenda Carroll, Charlie Anderson, Dave Cormack, Jon Kaplan, Steven H. King, Dave Markert, Jr., Dana Markert, Delaney Markert, Ken Runkel, Molly Faulk, George Miller, Greg and Gwen Duriez, Fred and Charlotte Miller, Fernando Nasmyth, Jeff and Suzie Parrow, Christopher and Shelia Sillitto, June and Scotty Witt, and Shane and Leah Bowen.

And there have been so many others who have encouraged me along the way, particularly mine and Jenny's extended families. Your support throughout our marriage has been superlative and your overt excitement about this project has gone so far to make it possible.

May our God bless you all.

SCREAMFREE™
RELATIONSHIP COACHING
Start a revolution in your life.

• Imagine relationships with your children led by your calmly chosen principles, even when your kids seem "out of control."

• Imagine an adventurous marriage guided by your pursuit of intimacy, even if you and your spouse cannot seem to "meet each other's needs."

• Imagine work relationships directed by own self-respect and quest for success, even if your workplace seems filled with politics and stagnation.

"Without hesitation I can tell you that Hal's ability to communicate and coach is beyond talent, it is a gift. Take the opportunity to start a coaching relationship with Hal; it will be the best thing you do for yourself and all your relationships. All I can say is that it left me asking, "Where has this guy been?!"

Tim King, President, Presence International

Your can revolutionize all your relationships. All it takes is a willingness to become ScreamFree.

Hal Edward Runkel, author, speaker, licensed family therapist, and visionary behind the ScreamFree approach to relationships, leads a team of coaches helping people all over the planet revolutionize their lives.

Don't hesitate to contact a ScreamFree Coach today. Your own ScreamFree revolution is waiting to begin. Contact us confidentially at coaching@screamfree.com or 1-800-760-0771 for a free 20-minute consultation.

The relationships you've always wanted are within your reach. Start a revolution in your life today.

SCREAMFREE™ LIVING
INCORPORATED
info@screamfree.com · 1-800-860-0771
www.screamfree.com

ATTEND A SCREAMFREE™ LIVE EVENT SOON!

Hal Runkel, author and creator of the revolutionary ScreamFree Living Series, along with his team of ScreamFree Living associates, presents live events in companies, churches, community centers, and schools throughout the US. Visit the web site at **www.screamfree.com** to learn about events near you, or if you don't see one in your location, contact us at **events@screamfree.com** to schedule an event at your organization.

We currently offer events and seminars in the following focus areas:

ScreamFree Parenting. Our flagship book and seminar series is revolutionizing the way parents respond to and relate with their kids. ScreamFree Parenting creates parents who are calm, cool, and *conn*ected with their kids. Attend one of our events and experience what parents are calling "a genuine, life-changing event."

ScreamFree Marriage. ScreamFree Marriage presents a refreshingly new understanding of your most intimate relationship, inspiring you to calm down, grow up and get closer to your spouse. Build a mature and profound love based on your own self respect and individual responsibility. You'll actually celebrate your differences as a foundation for a fulfilling and intimate relationship.

ScreamFree Leadership. ScreamFree Leadership inspires individuals, teams and organizations to operate at the peak of efficiency, productivity, and passion. By developing in each team member a profound understanding of how relationship systems really work, ScreamFree Leadership enables each individual to take hold of his/her own emotional reactivity and truly become the calming authority every organization needs.

Custom seminar available at your location.
Contact us today.

SCREAMFREE™ LIVING
INCORPORATED

info@screamfree.com · 1-800-860-0771
www.screamfree.com

Put ScreamFree™ *Parenting into Practice!*
FREE eBOOKS

Are you ready to continue the ScreamFree Parenting journey?
Select one or more of the following FREE eBook titles that
apply the valuable and proven ScreamFree Principles to
some common parenting challenges:

- *ScreamFree Birthday Parties*
- *ScreamFree First Day of School*
- *ScreamFree Summer Vacation*
- *ScreamFree Holidays*
- *ScreamFree College Search*

Send an email to ebooks@screamfree.com, and we'll send you a link to a page
containing these valuable FREE ebooks. Indicate which ones you're interested in.

If you would like a hard copy, send $6.95 for shipping and handling and $1.00 for each
eBook to:

ScreamFree Living Free eBooks   (Include postal address,
1180 Satellite Blvd, Suite 300   phone no., and email
Duluth, GA 30097   address and/or fax no.)

FREE eNEWSLETTER AND
ONLINE PARENTING FORUM

More practical ScreamFree Parenting
stories, tips, and news FREE! Help your
parenting journey with a free newsletter
from ScreamFree Living.
To register, go to www.screamfree.com
or email newsletter@screamfree.com.

Our web site also offers other products
including books, audio programs, and a free
ScreamFree Community Forum where you
can share your parenting stories and questions,
and learn from other parents who are on the
ScreamFree journey.

SCREAMFREE™ LIVING
I N C O R P O R A T E D
info@screamfree.com · 1-800-860-0771
www.screamfree.com